THE BOOK OF PRAYERS
Learning to Pray Covenant Prayers

DR. STEPHEN R. PHINNEY

Dedicated to my wife:
Janie Marie
My prayer partner for life!
For without my beloved wife, I would be
a man of prayerlessness.

An iPrint of Identity Matters Publishers

THE HOLY WORD OF GOD
Unless otherwise noted, all Scripture quotations are taken from the New American Standard Bible (NASB), ⓔ Copyright 1960, 1962, 1963, 1968, 1971, 1972, 1973, 1975, 1977, 1975 by the Lockman Foundation. Used by permission. Scripture quotations marked NKJV are taken from the New King James Version. Copyright © 1982 by Thomas Nelson, Inc. Used by permission. All rights reserved.

Book of Prayers – Learning To Pray Covenant Prayers
Copyright © 2007, 2009, 2013 & Revised 2021

ISBN: 978-1-300-48233-8
Imprint: Lulu.com
IOM America
P.O. Box 71
Sterling, Kansas 67579
(602) 292-2982
IOMAmerica.net
corporate@iomamerica.org

Library of Congress Cataloging-in-Publication Data
Phinney, Stephen Ray
Book of Prayers /by Dr. Stephen R. Phinney.

© 2021
Identity Matters Publishers | LuLu
Cover Design: Inphinnety Designs
Editing: IOM America
Sterling, KS

FORWARD

"Brevity is the soul of wit (wisdom)," said Shakespeare (parentheses added). [1] It is true in the Book of Prayers, authored by Dr. Stephen R. Phinney of IOM America. It can be easily read through in one sitting, but it is worth reading over and over again, as well as practicing constantly. Indeed, I am grateful to Dr. Phinney for inviting me to write a Foreword to the present edition. What a privilege it is.

In this project, he has gained us in debt to him for his admonition, exhortation, counsel, and challenge. At the outset, the author introduces the reader to the reality of every born-again indwelt person as involved in a lifelong struggle against the devil and the forces of evil. He asserts the biblical Truth that the Word of God and prayer are the two sure tools to fight the battle and emerge triumphantly. Fear and unhealthy fascination with Satan and his domain are fatal, he warns. Steve bases the book's content on his approach to the Scriptures, which he affirms as God-breathed, infallible, and authoritative on the belief and behavior of the Christian.

Dr. Phinney's focus on the New Covenant is spot on. As he states, "New Covenant living starts with covenant prayers."

A survey of the Contents pages show that the entire book is devoted to suggesting model prayers suitable to various specific needs and occasions, grouped under various titles, such as **General Warfare, Praying the Armor, Deeds of the Flesh, Family Life,** and **Prayer for Ministries and Leaders** - making the title, **Book of Prayers**, realistic. Several subtopics may surprise the reader, as they deal with areas of life most people hardly consider to be included in their prayer. Thus, this book is an eye-opener.

The study of this book may initiate people to consider strange and new topics to be included in their prayers; thus, enriching their personal prayer.

The Affirmation Prayer section presents a theology of prayer interspersed with befitting Bible quotes. Let me repeat - the whole book is thoroughly based on the Bible, which Steve asserts as the inspired, infallible, and authoritative Word of God. Any other standpoint should be judged as defective.

The section on Scriptures includes Bible quotes on faith, love, praise, obedience, fleshly mind, grace, Holy Spirit, faithfulness, Bride of Christ, and stewardship. These serve as challenges for topical study.

The last dit of the text on The Victor will assist in the self-evaluation of the users of this book.

The list of books in Recommended Reading will prove very helpful for those who continue the study for enhancing spiritual growth. I would strongly recommend the serious reader, and student start reading on page 96 - About the Ministry of IOM America. It will give the proper orientation to the reader as to the author's focus and target audience.

Your decision to read this book is commendable. May God bless you to improve your communication with Him.

Professor P. P. Thomas
Grace Counseling Center, India

[1] Quote from Hamlet, Act 2, Scene 2, by William Shakespeare, public domain.

CONTENTS	PAGE
INTRODUCTION	
First Things First	9
Marriage of The Lamb	15
Importance of Covenant Prayers	28
PERMISSIBLE SUFFOCATION	48
The Elements of Pain	62
Engaging Our Sufferings	71
GENERAL WARFARE	76
Selfer's Prayer	77
Victory	80
Protection	81
Repentance	82
Mental Protection	84
Forgiving Others	85
How to Extend Forgiveness	87
How to Seek Forgiveness	89
Acts of Rebellion	91
Renouncing Pride	93
Renouncing Sexual Bonds	95
Sinful Habits	97
Sins of Forefathers	99
Prayer for Illness	101
Sensing an Evil Spirit	103
Affirming Salvation	105
Relational Walls	107
Death of a Loved One	109
PRAYING THE ARMOR	111
Belt of Truth	112
Righteousness	113

Peace	114
Faith	115
The Sword	116
Salvation	117
Full Armor	119
Aggressive Warfare	122
Praying Armor Onto Others	123

DEEDS OF THE FLESH   125

Flesh	126
Adultery	128
Fornication	129
Uncleanness	131
Sensuality	132
Idolatry	134
Stubbornness	136
Hatred	138
Quarreling	139
Jealousy	141
Anger	143
Arguing	145
Bad Doctrines	147
Envy	149
Temptation of Murder	151
Bathing in Sin	153

PRAYING FOR OTHERS   155

Warfare for Others	156
Prayer for Marriages	158
Family Life Prayers	159
Prayer for Parents	160
Prayer for Children	162
Prayer for Grandchildren	164
Seeing Evil Images	166
Fear of Losing a Child	168

Prayer for Single Parents	**170**
Protection at Bedtime	**171**
Quarreling Between Children	**173**
Children's Fascination with Violence	**175**
Children Attracted to the Occult	**177**
Early Sensual Attractions	**179**
Child Sexual Perversions	**180**
Out of Control Children	**181**
PRAYER FOR LEADERSHIP	**182**
Prayers for Leaders	**183**
Prayer for Ministry	**185**
Affirmation Prayer	**187**
VICTORY IN CHRIST	**190**
Special Note from the Author	
SCRIPTURES OF HELP	**196**
Faith	
Love	
Praise	
Obedience	
Fleshly Mind	
Grace	
Holy Spirit	
Faithfulness	
Bride of Christ	
Stewardship	
THE AUTHOR'S LIFE MISSION	**209**
RECOMMENDED READING	**211**

INTRODUCTION
Book of Prayers – Learning To Pray Covenant Prayers

FIRST THINGS FIRST

"Then I heard something like the voice of a great multitude and like the sound of many waters and like the sound of mighty peals of thunder, saying, 'Hallelujah! For the Lord our God, the Almighty, reigns. Let us rejoice and be glad and give the glory to Him, for the marriage of the Lamb has come and His bride has made herself ready.' It was given to her to clothe herself in fine linen, bright and clean; for the fine linen is the righteous acts of the saints. Then he said to me, 'Write, "Blessed are those who are invited to the marriage supper of the Lamb."' And he said to me, 'These are true words of God.' Then I fell at his feet to worship him. But he said to me, 'Do not do that; I am a fellow servant of yours and your brethren who hold the testimony of Jesus; worship God. For the testimony of Jesus is the spirit of prophecy.'" **Revelation 19:6-10**

Before I offer the practical samples of praying New Covenant prayers, we need to understand the Groom's role—Jesus Christ and His Bride—the true indwelt believers who house the Holy Spirit living within them, which we call authentic believers.

It is all about the marriage of Jesus Christ!

The perfect description of Covenant Marriage is best described in the Book of Revelation. However, the meaning, purpose, description is found from Genesis to Revelation's book. I believe the ordained reason for creation, Old Covenant (Old Testament), the New Covenant (New Testament), and the Book of Revelation is given to us to secure a Bride for God the Father's Son – Jesus.

In looking at the Revelation 19:6-10, the voice John had heard earlier forbidding him to record the seven peals of thunder's words spoke to him once again. As he had earlier, John again became an active participant in this vision. Remember that he left the place of an observer to become an actor in this drama.

God the Father was giving John the "heartbeat" of the "why" He created the earth, allowed the fall of man, delivered a redeemer, and offered Covenant Marriage to all those who received the indwelling Life of Christ through salvation – through the filling of the Holy Spirit.

You must understand the two types of marriages. The first is the Covenant Marriage represented in Heaven that is the ONLY anointed marriage system God supports. The second is marriage certificates that were fabricated or established by the governing laws of nations. Proof of this is in the modality of why you need a license from the state/nation – along with a signature of an "ordained" church leader.

One of the misnomers of governed marriages is – *God supports all marriages sealed by a governing state or nation*. He does not. If He did, it would erase His ordinances of Covenant Marriage. Plus, all current legal marriages between dogs and their masters, adult-minor marriages, same-sex marriages, or any other culturally friendly marriages would be ordained/accepted by God. That would be heresy.

The Authentic Mission of the Bride & Groom

In John's experience of being *caught up into Heaven*, the Lord delivers this message to write.

"You must prophesy again concerning many peoples and nations and tongues and kings."

With God refueling his commission, John was about to embrace the most horrific but glorious reveals of all. He's being reminded to be faithful to his service to write with the passion of Christ. What God was about to reveal to him would affect every life that was and is to come—the marriage of the Lamb. We are about to enter some of the most avoided scriptures in the entire Bible, passages that have been argued over since the day of John. No matter what your "theological bent" is—one thing is clear; when John writes the standards of Covenant Marriage, the domain of Satan, his demons, and his persecuting followers will be broken, and the opinions of mankind will matter not. Each will be forced with the authentic doctrines of the "why" God created the earth – to handpick Bridal members for His Son. All who have dishonored God by violating His Eternal Covenant Marriage guidelines will be rightly dealt with (judged) for every thought, attitude, governing law, and action that has risen against the ordained reasoning for Covenant Marriages.

Saying "Goodbye" to the ideologies of ungodly/worldly marriages, God is about to take ownership of what has always belonged to Him – the perfection of marriages made in Heaven. Before we review the details of Covenant Marriages, let's take a look at the pathway of the Groom.

The planet is His—always has been. It was created for Him to establish a breeding ground to produce a Bride for His Son, Jesus. The masses that do not understand the Groom's full pathway will most likely read this as a bit odd. Let's review the pathway of the Groom.

OLD TESTAMENT MARRIAGE

God formed the earth for His benefit. He then established Hebrew Law (characteristics of God) for daily living—we call this the Old Testament. Hebrew law descends from Heaven; men do not make it up. Therefore, it is a Holy act to study and embrace Hebrew Law, culture, and customs. Contained within Hebrew domestic Laws, it is required for the firstborn male to marry. It is not optional. The firstborn male is he who inherits all of the ways of the father. It is what guarantees the stability of multigenerational family life. It also preserves the character of God in culture. Due to this fact and the reality that God Himself obeys His own Hebrew Laws, He formed or created a system to reproduce itself (Genesis 1:22), filling the stockyard. Why? For the Father to handpick the "cream of the crop" as Bridal Members for His Son.

Critical Note: The Hebrew tithing requirement of 10% is based on this "cream of the crop" concept. Many Christians believe the percentages related to the narrow and wide gate are these Hebrew tithing percentages. I happen to be one of those that believe this.

"Enter through the narrow gate; for the gate is wide and the way is broad, leading to destruction, and there are many who enter through it. For the gate is small and the way is narrow that leads to life, and there are few who find it." (Matthew 7:13-14)

There's a good chance that God Himself would reveal the fact that 10% of the entire population, from Genesis 1:1 to the last verse in the book of Revelation, would be this 10%.

Here is our reality. God created the earth, and all that is in it, to set the stage for picking Bridal Members for His Son. He formed the garden, established the two trees, put Satan in the tree of knowledge, set Adam and Eve up for a choice, and then allowed the fall, which was all a part of the selective process. That puts a completely different slant on why God created us. For years I believed that we humans had put too much of a selfish bent on why God made us. When I hear some of the warm and fuzzy Biblically wrong reasons for our existence, I am overwhelmed with compassion. So much so, I am compelled to share the righteous reasons for the existence of humanity.

When we look at culture today, we see those percentages flipped. People think that true Christianity is Christ-following—that's probably more like 90% of the people, particularly in this county, but most likely, people worldwide think that they are true authentic Christians, which simply does not work with Hebrew Law or cus-toms.

The Old Testament was when God established His mandates and guidelines for His Son's future marriage; it was done by releasing the Hebrew Law on the earth. It was also a time when Jesus stayed in Heaven while His Father did what Father's do—prepared the way for His Son.

MARRIAGE MADE IN HEAVEN

"After these things, I heard something like a loud voice of a great multitude in heaven, saying, 'Hallelujah! Salvation and glory and power belong to our God; BECAUSE HIS JUDGMENTS ARE TRUE AND RIGHTEOUS; for He has judged the great harlot who was corrupting the earth with her immorality, and HE HAS AVENGED THE BLOOD OF HIS BOND-SERVANTS ON HER.' And a second time, they said, 'Hallelujah! HER SMOKE RISES UP FOREVER AND EVER.' And the twenty-four elders and the four living creatures fell down and worshiped God who sits on the throne saying, 'Amen. Hallelujah!' And a voice came from the throne, saying, 'Give praise to our God, all you His bond-servants, you who fear Him, the small and the great.' Then I heard something like the voice of a great multitude and like the sound of many waters and like the sound of mighty peals of thunder, saying, 'Hallelujah! For the Lord our God, the Almighty, reigns. Let us rejoice and be glad and give the glory to Him, for the marriage of the Lamb has come and His bride has made herself ready.' It was given to her to clothe herself in fine linen, bright and clean; for the

fine linen is the righteous acts of the saints. Then he said to me, 'Write, "Blessed are those who are invited to the marriage supper of the Lamb.'" And he said to me, 'These are true words of God.' Then I fell at his feet to worship him. But he said to me, 'Do not do that; I am a fellow servant of yours and your brethren who hold the testimony of Jesus; worship God. For the testimony of Jesus is the spirit of prophecy.'" Revelation 19:1-10

THE MYSTERY OF THE HARLOT

Have you ever wondered why the enemy (Satan), his government (Babylon), and his religious leader (False Prophet) are almost always referenced as a harlot and immoral? Not only have I been curious about this, but I have also done years of study regarding this mystery. My conclusion is rather simple. Since the whole point of creation and all that occurs up to this chapter is mostly about God securing a Bride for His Son, Satan's goal has been and will continue to be that of developing immorality in the world — defiling the marriage bed. He thinks by doing this to the human force; he is defiling the marriage bed of Christ.

The final announcement of great Babylon being destroyed or that it has fallen and that it is time for all of Heaven to rejoice is exactly what is happening here in our passage. I often feel bad for the Universalists because their whole mission is to turn God into a lukewarm God who would never rejoice over destruction. Do you see how that ideology rubs in the face of God's righteous judgments? Not only should the Bride of Christ be "OK" with God shouting praises over His judgments, but we should also join Him. Keep in mind that He gave some 6,000 years of warnings and invites to these lukewarm Universalists. At this point in our passage, the time is not only up, but the antichrist system has been destroyed, and now they are rejoicing in Heaven because of it.

ETERNAL SMOKE OFFERING

As for Babylon's burning and its smoke that darkens the Heavens, if you do a proper study on this, you will discover that the burning of Babylon is like an eternal smoke-offering raising itself into eternity to remind all who are in Heaven of the great and mighty judgment of God, and this why He says, "Hallelujah! Her smoke rises forever and ever." Why are these 24 elders and four living creatures bowing down and worshipping God over Babylon's burning? It is because God just destroyed the force, structure, and religious whoredom that has afflicted His Son's Bride for generations. At this point in our journey, she is free from all temptations, defilements, and tortures that Satan has afflicted on the woman (Bride of Christ)—from the tyranny of God's greatest enemy.

Coming from my finite mind, you can believe that there will be "the sound of many waters and like the sound of mighty peals of thunder saying, 'Hallelujah! For the Lord our God, the Al-mighty, reigns.'" The God of the true universe has freed His Son's Bride eternally.

THE MARRIAGE OF THE LAMB

"Let us rejoice and be glad and give the glory to Him, for the marriage of the Lamb has come and His bride has made herself ready. It was given to her to clothe herself in fine linen, bright and clean; for the fine linen is the righteous acts of the saints." (Revelation 19:7-8)

Allow me to share with you some of the basic facts regarding Hebrew marriage.

Looking at Hebrews 13:4, it says, "Marriage is to be held in honor among all, and the marriage bed is to be undefiled; for fornicators and adulterers God will judge." This is a serious statement coming to us from the Word of God. When we look at marriage today, we see everything from marrying your dog to marrying your same-sex boyfriend.

Marriage is to be held in high honor by all, but its objective in this passage states that "honor" is to be shown to marriage as an institution. It is not to be undervalued as though celibacy were purer. Any violation of the marriage contract should not dishonor it. It means the "contract" established between a man and a woman is a "covenant" sealed in Heaven. What God joins in a union, no man or his laws can separate. Matthew 19:6 says, "So they are no longer two, but one flesh. What therefore God has joined together let no man separate." When mankind devalues the marriage institution, they are subtly attacking the "marriage of the Lamb." For God, the Father of Jesus Christ, gave us the institution of marriage to demonstrate, by law and relationship, what is to come with His Son.

HISTORY OF MARRIAGE

Marriage was instituted in the Garden of Eden when man was in his innocence (Genesis 2:18-24). Here we have its original contract, confirmed by the Lord, as the basis on which all laws and marital guidelines are to be framed (Mat-thew 19:4-5). Monogamy (one spouse until death) was the original design of marriage (Matthew 19:5; 1 Corinthians 6:16). This design was violated early on when man's problems with lust began to overflow into God's ordinances of marriage (Genesis 4:19; 6:2). We meet the occurrence of polygamy (two or more wives) and concubinage (a wife of secondary rank) in the patriarchal age (Genesis 16:1-4; 22:21-24). Polygamy was recognized in the Mosaic Law, made its way into legislation, and continued to be practiced through Jewish history until their captivity to Egypt, after which there is no instance of it on record.

Why is all this significant? The lust of our forefathers wanting plurality of wives did not have the option of divorce because divorce did not exist. Therefore, they instituted polygamy and concubinage to fulfill their appetites for trying out different women. The leadership of the day "buckled" under the pressure of the men and legislated their lust. Polygamy and concubinage were the entrance or gateway for divorce. Shortly after the legislation of polygamy, divorce was instituted to keep God's laws of monogamy. In the eyes of our forefathers, this became the new and legal way to fulfill the lust of their flesh.

HISTORY OF DIVORCE

If we do not understand the history of divorce, we will not be able to embrace the words of Jesus when the "religious leaders" of His day were testing Him with the laws of Moses. Matthew 19:3 tells us this: "Some Pharisees came to Jesus, testing Him and asking, 'Is it lawful for a man to divorce his wife for any reason at all?'" Jesus' response was consistent with history. "And He answered and said, 'Have you not read that He who created them from the beginning MADE THEM MALE AND FEMALE,' and said, 'FOR THIS REASON A MAN SHALL LEAVE HIS FATHER AND MOTHER AND BE JOINED TO HIS WIFE, AND THE TWO SHALL BECOME ONE FLESH? So they are no longer two, but one flesh. What therefore God has joined together let no man separate" (Matthew 9:4-6). The statement "let no man separate" is translated out as "let no man's law separate." The other significant statement made here is "from the beginning." Their reasons for satisfying their lust did not catch Jesus's attention. He simply went back to His Father's design of monogamy (one wife until death).

SATAN'S PURPOSE FOR DIVORCE

Now the big question: Why would the enemy push so hard for legislating divorce? Another simple answer: Because if the enemy can break up the original design of "one woman + one man + one Father = one flesh," he would then be able to in-grain into the hearts of man that just maybe, "One Father + One Son + One Spirit does not equal One God." That is nothing short of one of his biggest lies. Secondly, he would convince the Bride of Christ that there is a possibility Christ would forsake or divorce His Bride. Divorce is the human tool used by the enemy to try to break up the Trinity in the hearts of man. Divorce needs to be viewed through the eyes of God first and, secondly, through history. This is man's futile attempt to legislate lust and also a refusal to reconcile. Since the whole mission and purpose of Jesus Christ is to reconcile the people back to God, Satan has used this misnomer of divorce to put doubts in the minds of humanity. People do tend to view God as and through the way they behave. God the Father ordained the institution of marriage to set in concrete for mankind the fundamental Truth of "One Father + One Son + One Spirit = One God."

THE FATHER'S VIEW OF MARRIAGE

The charter of marriage is in Genesis 2:24, reproduced by our Lord with great distinctness as is found in Matthew 19:4-5. God the Father, God the Son, and God the Holy Spirit are all separate individual beings but are One as a whole. God the Father established the institution of marriage in the Gar-den to prepare the way for the original eternal design and un-ion of Christ and the Church (Eph. 5:31; Mark 10:5-9; 1 Cor. 6:16; 7:2). The point is this: The husband and wife, united in marriage, combine to form one perfect human being, complement and be a completer of the other. Therefore, Christ makes the Church a necessary appendage of Himself. He is the model from whom, as the blueprint, the Church is formed (Romans 6:5). As the husband is of the wife, he is her Head, her governing authority, her protector. Death is the only tool that severs the bridegroom and the bride, but death cannot separate Christ and His bride. If you look at the reality that we need to be brought unto the end—death to the self-life; this principle—Hebrew law, remains in play. Our death is what unites us to Him (Romans 8).

"This mystery is great, but I am speaking with reference to Christ and the church" (Ephesians 5:32).

In this passage, the phrase "the mystery is great" is the Truth—hidden once but now revealed. Christ's spiritual union with the Church is mysteriously represented by marriage—not marriage in the general sense, but the marriage of Christ and the Church. Paul said, *"For we are members of His [glorified] body, of His flesh and of His bones"* (Ephesians 5:30). This statement should sound a bit familiar to you. When Adam was placed into a deep sleep, the Father formed Eve out of his open side, symbolizing Christ's death, which was the birth of His spouse, the Church. As Adam gave Eve a new name, so Christ gives the Church His new name. "He who has an ear, let him hear what the Spirit says to the churches. To him who overcomes, to him, I will give some of the hidden manna, and I will give him a white stone, and a new name written on the stone which no one knows but he who receives it" (Revelation 2:17). That is the Hebrew reason why the woman takes on a new name. She has to shed the name of her father and adopt the name and lineage of her husband.

Neither the Bible (in general) nor Jesus (in particular) treat the family from the point of view of a historian or sociologist, but solely from that of a teacher of the Father's principles and morals. In short, their point of view is "Godological" (theological) rather than sociological. Moses and the prophets, no less than Jesus and His apostles, accepted marriage as a holy institution that gave rise to certain practical, ethical questions, and they dealt with them accordingly. There is nothing in the record of the teachings of

Jesus and His apostles to indicate that they "caved in" to marital, social content, cus-toms, or sanctions. They accepted it as God's conventional, civilized ways for His people. They also accepted its connected customs, which were for ethical and illustrative purposes. There is one exception to this general statement: Je-sus acknowledged, because of the demands of social development, for Moses to modify the law permitting and regulating divorce. At the same time, this indicates that He regarded such modifications as out of harmony with the institution that God the Father established for the Hebrew people. According to the original divine purpose, marriage was monogamous. Any form of polygamy, and apparently of divorce, was excluded from His Father's divine idea and purpose, which is why Jesus was taking them back to "in the beginning." Many modern believers use Jesus's Word in Matthew 19 as an excuse or permission for divorce, which could not be farther from the Truth. His statement to the religious leaders of that day was a correction of "straying from the beginning." For if Jesus had put a hardy approval on divorce that day, He would have subtly allowed a "cheap" doctrine of forsaking His bride.

THE FATHER CHOOSES THE BRIDE

It is not a popular idea, particularly in our society today, to have our fathers pick bridal members for our sons. Somewhere throughout the original Hebrew into the modern Hebrew, this Hebraic tradition faded into governing societies. Now, the only people who seem to understand the importance of a father picking a bridal member for his son are the Orthodox Jews. They understand exactly what I am going to be talking about.

Divorce is as common as changing your shoes. People today seem to be so focused on being happy that they do not work through the reconciliation issues, which come with most marriages. That is too bad, though! The "enduring to the end" scripture, which is mentioned throughout the New Testament, relates directly to the issue of the Bride of Jesus Christ. Imagine for a moment that Jesus was not faithful in enduring to the end with us. Would we expect Him to divorce us because of our unfaithfulness? I hope not! This topic will challenge most believers to the core. At least, that has been my experience in discipling couples in my office.

It is sad to realize that most "Christians" have no clue what our passage is saying. The fact is, the entire process of the Old and New Testament, which is now being explained to us in the book of Revelation, is all about the Father choosing the Bride for His Son and preparing her for this moment found in our passage.

Even though it is not a popular idea today, Hebrew tradition reveals the groom's father played a significant role in "pick-ing" a bride for his son. That is not only the case with God the Father and Jesus Christ His Son, but this was a tradition, which God required of the Hebrew people. The father looked for economic, social, and spiritual qualities, as well as a pure bloodline. These elements were important for the father because these qualities would preserve his investments. It took the wisdom of a father to look through the son's desires of the flesh to marry and assist him in finding a bride who would be suitable as a helpmate and life-giver. Keep in mind that all marriages are for the lineage before them; it helps preserve the spiritual beliefs and the investment that the father made for the generations. The father was simply interested in protecting his investment for his son and that his son would pass this down to his eldest son. A wise father understood that a woman could take all that away in a short period. Since the purpose of a father's life was to "set up" the next generation to manage his inheritance (rewards of his investments and labor), he made sure his son had a wife who would not squander it (Exodus 34:16). It was the father's responsibility to form his son's future and then teach him how to do the same with his sons. We call it the spiritual generation inheritance, while most people keep it locked up in the walls of physical inheritance.

Another significant point is that a young man typically looked at the outward beauty of a woman as the primary qualification to marry her, while the father looked at the inward beauty. It took these two elements together to get a qualified bride. Because young men lack experience, they tend to look at a woman externally. Older men, men of wisdom, understand that external beauty quickly fades away; the man is then left with the inward woman, and many times that wasn't much. Therefore, the son had to have complete trust in his father and assist him in doing the "picking."

Let it be known that a son had the right to look and desire, but the father is the one who did the choosing. Judges 14:2 shows us this: "So he came back and told his father and mother, 'I saw a woman in Timnah, one of the daughters of the Philistines; now, therefore, get her for me as a wife.'" The simple point here is that the son knew he could not obtain the woman independently—it required the father to "work the deal" for him.

DEFINITION OF BETROTHED

Betroth (אָרַשׂ,'āras) derives from the word "troth" or the Hebrew word of Truth (' אֱמֶתĕmeth). The literal meaning here is to "be" engaged in "trooth." This explains the critical reason why the parents were diligently in the "negotiations of dowry" to discover the Truth of the groom, his family, the bride, and her family. When you are married, you marry tribes, and tribes have traditions and beliefs that affected the couple for generations to come.

Another critical factor is that you were sealed for marriage once you were "betrothed," according to Hebrew law. That means if you decided to "end" the relationship during the engagement, you would have to go through the divorce process. In the story of Joseph getting ready to "send her [Mary] away" (because of her pregnancy of Jesus), God had to send an angel to tell Joseph it was a supernatural conception by God. The term "put her away" if you get into the Greek codex of this passage, you'll discover it is the same Word used "to divorce her." The great mystery is that once you were engaged to someone, you had started the marriage process. You had to wait one year before a marriage supper, which bound the couple together by the fathers because they had to make sure she was pure.

"Now the birth of Jesus was as follows: when His mother Mary had been betrothed to Joseph before they came together, she was found to be with child by the Holy Spirit. And Joseph, her husband, being a righteous man and not wanting to disgrace her, planned to send her away secretly. But when he had considered this, behold, an angel of the Lord appeared to him in a dream, saying. 'Joseph, son of David, do not be afraid to take Mary as your wife; for the Child who has been conceived in her is of the Holy Spirit" (Matthew 1:18-20).

The parallel is this: when Jesus accepted us for Salvation, He agreed to become engaged or "betrothed" to us. The actual wedding has not occurred yet, which is what the Second Coming of Christ is for; even more meticulously, the Rapture to come and get His Bride. But after the Bride is raptured up, we remain in waiting until Jesus comes in His Second Com-ing, permanently punishing Satan, his triune, and all those who followed him. Once all that has been completed, there will be a marriage supper, and that is what our passage is talking about.

The engagement phase with Christ is where we are right now living on the earth. Christ is waiting to see who endures to the end—what bridal members (who are engaged) keep oil in their lamps. He is "cleaning us up" and preparing us for His Wedding. Ephesians 5:27 says, "That He might present to Himself the church in all her glory, having no spot or wrinkle or any such thing; but that she would be holy and blameless." Our "betrothment" period with Christ is for the "working out of our salvation" (Philippians 2:12).

Here is the point: the engagement period is a promise "by one's truth" to fulfill the process of preparing for marriage, which usually took place a year or more before marriage. From the time of betrothal, the woman was regarded as the lawful wife of the man she was betrothed (Deuteronomy 28:30; Judges 14:2,8; Matthew 1:18-21). The idea is figuratively representative of the spiritual connection between God and His people (Hosea 2:9-20). In this great parable of the prodigal wife, Hosea uses betrothal as the symbol of God the Father and how He pledged His love and favor to Israel. Since we are grafted into the Hebrew (Jewish) bloodline, this principle also applies to us (Romans 11:23). At the point of Hosea's betrothal (engagement) to Gomer, she was a whore (an unclean woman who gives herself away to "men of the covenant"). Like Gomer, we, too, are a "mess." Many of us act like whores. I know that sounds rather blunt, but it is true. Being the mess that we are, when Christ decides to "betroth" Himself to us, it becomes one of the greatest miracles stated in the Bible throughout history. However, the good news is that He takes the engagement period to "clean us up" by washing through and with His blood with the Word and releasing the Holy Spirit within us to fulfill His Father's mandates.

THE NEGOTIATIONS OF ENGAGEMENT

Genesis 34:6-17 is profound. The passage is one of the clearest Hebrew pictures of the betrothal process. The situation here is that Prince Shechem lusted after one of Jacob's daughters (Dinah). He took her to the field and had sex with her. Her protective brothers found out about it, and now we have the betrothal process. Note: Even though the situation here is grim, the process of engagement is quite clear.

It all starts with a conference, as such, between the parental parties. As in the case with Hamor, the father of Shechem (son of lust), and Jacob (the father of Dinah), the parents on both sides are the principals of authority in the negotiation. The sons of Jacob, being brothers of the injured damsel, are present according to custom. The actions were to check out any deeds contrary to sanctity, which God's holy people must characterize. Hamor makes his restitution proposal; he proposes a political alliance or merger of the two tribes, to be sealed and affected by intermarriage. He offers to make them joint possessors of the soil and the rights of dwelling, trading, and acquiring property.

Shechem now speaks with respect and sincerity. He offers any dowry, bridal presents, and gifts to the mother and brothers of the bride. It must be acknowledged that the father and the son were inclined to make whatever amends they could for the grievous offense that had been committed. The sons of Jacob answered as a representative of their father, and they responded with the following conditions of giving Jacob's daughter over to Shechem. They said that they could not intermarry with the uncircumcised; only on the condition that every male was circumcised would they consent (Genesis 34:14-15). On these terms, the father and son promised to "become one people" with the "bride's" Hebrew race and traditions.

Even though Jacob's sons used this dowry to kill Shechem and his people, the negotiation process reveals engagement traditions. The price for Shechem's bride was death; he didn't realize it at the time. It is amazing how one of the most fleshly and deceptive stories in the Bible reveals the way of God the Father—the Hebrew traditions.

God the Father, of the Son to be "betrothed," had to negotiate with "the father of lies" to retain the bride for His Son. Think about that—the price was His Son's life. Like Hosea, He had to come and take on the sins of the bride-to-be, take the punishment for those sins, and then open His arms for engagement. He again, like Hosea, had to "put up with" the betrothed bride who was still a whore—going back to her sins of preference until the day of sanctification. Well, if you know the story of Hosea, you know that Gomar makes several trips back to her old lifestyle, very much the Christians of today. God required Hosea, and Christ, to be the ones responsible for the "cost" of "engagement" while releasing the "betrothed" or the bride-to-be from the consequences of her actions. God knows that the full price of dowry falls on the Groom because He is the One who set the rules of engagement. In this case, the dowry was death for Jesus. Secondly, He was responsible for making sure the Bride was ready for the wedding day. Once the Bride was purified and ready, He would come for her. In our case, that is the Rapture first — the point of removal of the Bridal members, and the Great Wed-ding Feast, which is the covenant made by God the Father in Heaven to unite Jesus Christ with His Bride.

I cannot tell you how much fun it is to explore the laws, customs, and manners of Hebrew marriage. It is one of my favorite things to do!

As we learned earlier, the engagement period for the Hebrew people was for one full year. When the year had passed and the room (normally an addition onto the father's house prepared by the groom) was finished, the groom would come for his bride— typically in the middle of the night. Neither the bride nor her parents were privy to either the day or the hour. She had to be always ready. The reason why this needed to be a surprise visit is that sin tends to cause people to manipulate and "fake it until they make it." The groom would announce to his father that he had finished his work. The father would inspect the work, give his approval, and the son would then go to get his bride. The groom's parents would stay behind to prepare for the arrival of their son and his bride. The groom would approach the home of the bride and call her out. The bride's father had to submit to the hour and grant his daughter the right of passage to her husband. The bride would come to the door dressed in her wedding attire and veil. At this point, the veil was taken off and laid on the shoulder of the bridegroom, and this declaration was made: "The government shall be upon his shoulder" (remember that in Hebrew tradition, a patriarch's authority was the same a government). The groom now accepted the responsibility of his new, little kingdom.

A procession would set out from the bride's home to the place the groom had prepared for his new, little kingdom. The pathway to their new home would be lit with oil lamps held by wedding guests. In the story told by Jesus, the bride and groom were later than expected, so the oil in the lamps began to run low. Only those who had brought a reserve flask of oil were able to refill their lamps and welcome the bride and groom (Matthew 25:1-13). There was singing and music along the way (Jeremiah 16:9), and sometimes, the bride herself would join in the dancing because of her excitement of the hour.

God makes a big deal about the wedding process. He makes a big deal about the engagement process, and He certainly makes a big deal about choosing the right woman.

JESUS THE BRIDEGROOM

"Then the kingdom of heaven will be comparable to ten virgins who took their lamps and went out to meet the bridegroom" (Matthew 25:1).

The coming of Christ (to receive His people to Himself) is often represented by the likeness of a marriage, with the Church representing His spouse or bride. The marriage relationship is the most tender, firm, and endearing of any known on the earth, and on this account, it rightfully represents the union of believers to Christ (Matthew 9:15; John 3:29; Revelation 19:7; 21:9; Ephesians 5:25-32). Read, study, and discover how profound God uses the marriage institution as a clear picture of what is taking place in the book of Revelation.

Ten virgins—these virgins, without question, represent the Church. Virgin is the name given because it is pure and holy (2 Corinthians 11:2; Lamentations 1:15; 2:13). These virgins took their lamps and went forth to meet the bridegroom. The lamps used on such an occasion were torches. They were made by winding up rags around pieces of iron or pottery, sometimes hollowed out to contain oil, and fastened to wood handles. The torches were dipped in oil and gave out a lot of light. Marriage ceremonies in the East were conducted with great ritual and seriousness. Friends attended for both the bride and bridegroom. The engaged or betrothed was escorted in a seat carried on poles by four or more persons. After the marriage ceremony, there was a feast for seven days. The feast was celebrated in the father of the bride's house. At the end of that time, the bridegroom escorted the bride, with great pageantry and splendor, to the home he had prepared for her during the engagement. How cool is that?

THE IMPORTANCE OF COVENANT PRAYERS

Covenant prayers represent or present supplications in light of an appeal versus telling your Husband what to do. Since the New Covenant fulfilled the Old Covenant, the Bridal members of Jesus Christ need to pray in a fashion that expresses fulfillment instead of begging for changes or, in some cases, demanding that the everlasting God change eternity for the one praying. Simply put, Covenant prayers confirm New Covenant Truth.

Critical Note: While Covenant prayers are the most Biblically sound prayers you can pray, Satan will work tirelessly to turn your thanksgiving of hardships into an attitude of demanding.

DESENSITIZATION OF SATAN

Satan has successfully used the world, and all of its influences, to bring a light-hearted attitude and mindset regarding the kingdom of darkness. Just take a look at the enormous volume of books, movies, video games, T-shirts, music, toys, television, advertisements, the internet, fashions, jewelry, and, of course, silly jesting that we are bombarded with wherever we turn!

The desensitization about Satan and his role in man's sins is a subtle but strategic attack on God's divine creation – His blessed children. The enemy of this world sees that the world (his domain) laughs him off with indifference. Always remember this callousness is the most powerful tool the enemy has in defusing God's serious plan of redemption. Christians ought never to entertain crude joke making, purchase degrading media products, or lightheartedly support Satan in any way. Believers need to exercise care in not assigning all of their wrongdoing as Satan's responsibility. We must, with biblical insight, understand the limited power of Satan and his kingdom. Oppression and bondage are not joking matters.

The key in the believer's emphasis on spiritual warfare must be based on a biblical approach to the subject. Subjective feelings, emotional desires, and genuine sincerity are not sufficient weaponry against an enemy who laughs in the face of one's intents. He yields no ground to emotion or sincerity. He retreats only from the authority and power that has been given to the

Christian through his/her union with the Lord Jesus Christ and the absolute Truth of the Word of God. Is an illustration worth remembering is this: If I were to give you a sharp two-edged sword and a butter knife, which would you use to fight an assailant? Dumb question? I don't think so! Your logical male side would choose the sharp, two-edged sword. However, in reality, when we do not use the Word of God to fight off the enemy, we are essentially using a butter knife to war against an enemy who slings a ball and chain.

"Take . . . the sword of the Spirit, which is the word of God" (Ephesians 6:17b).

Satan hates the New Covenant, which is the fulfillment & release of the condemnation of the Old Covenant!

We have two basic offensive weapons to use against Satan. They are the Word of God, primarily the New Covenant, and the power of prayer. When we put the two of these together, we have the most intimidating weapon known to the enemy. He knows he has been "had" when a man of God masters the art of using the Word of God in the power of prayer.

I pray that you are beginning to see our critical need for the Word of God and prayer. The sword of the Spirit, God's Word, is living and active. These are not words on a page. They are life-giving Words from the mouth of a living God! Use our own words, and we die. Use God's Words, and we live. It's as simple as that!

"For the Word of God is living and active and sharper than any two-edged sword, and piercing as far as the division of soul and spirit, of both joints and marrow, and able to judge the thoughts and intentions of the heart" (Hebrews 4:12).

The Word is eternal just as God Himself is eternal. Just as God is omnipotent (all-powerful), so does His Word have all the needed power to defeat the enemy and to accomplish God's will. Just as God is immutable, so the Word of God will never change. Just as our Lord is omnipresent, so His Word is always there and ready to be used in every situation. Just as God is holy, so His Word is holy. The bottom line is this: His Word is living, active, and sharper than any two-edged sword. The enemy hates hearing it. Jesus used it to fight off temptation. We can't survive without it.

As a sword, the Word has the power to penetrate the life of every being who hears it, and that includes the enemy. It is meant to do corrective surgery within the soul, spirit, thoughts, attitudes, and body of all who hear it. This is the secret of its power against the enemy. As it is read/heard, the Word can penetrate, cleanse, and change the lives of those who embrace it as Truth. It is why it cuts away at the grip of the enemy. There is nothing more powerful, and there is certainly no substitute for persistent, steady, consistent application of coming against the enemy. Even Jesus, the Son of God, used the written Word in the wilderness to fight off Satan. What worked for the Son of the living God will certainly do no less for us!

"Jesus, full of the Holy Spirit, returned from the Jordan and was led around by the Spirit in the wilderness for forty days being tempted by the devil. And He ate nothing during those days, and when they had ended, He became hungry. And the devil said to Him, 'If You are the Son of God, tell this stone to become bread'" (Luke 4:1-3).

The importance of doctrinal Truth and doctrinal praying is given to us by God to use daily. Doctrine, God's unchanging Truth, is mighty in defeating our enemies. As Christians, this Truth must go deep into our hearts. This will only come about as we understand the Holy Word of God and then use that Word aggressively in our lives. The following material will help keep doctrinal Truth at the forefront of our warfare activities.

Normally speaking, I am not one who advocates following "steps" to embrace freedom. However, when it comes to deliverance from strongholds in our lives, I see a definite need for a plan. Faithfully following these suggestions, word-for-word, will equip us and build a foundation for our souls. The Holy Spirit will aggressively act to guard our hearts against our enemies.

WARNINGS

Whenever we go to the frontlines, where the enemy lives and breathes, he is bound to try chasing us away. Do not submit to his deceptive ideas and lies: there is no time; this level of combat isn't necessary; these are only words; we can put this off because we already have too many things to do; we're tired or too sick; or that we are already struggling with worries, doubts, and fears that will prevent us from completing our pathway to deliverance. We should push through it all and respond like warriors!

In rare cases, some people experience terrifying feelings of guilt, worthlessness, physical symptoms (choking, pains moving around the body, tightness above the eyes, dizziness, blackouts, or even fainting), and terrifying spells of panic and depression. If any of these symptoms occur to the point of "paralyzing" you from not being able to go through the study, you will need a spiritual mentor (male church leader) who understands balanced warfare to pray over you. Remember, fear is the fire from the dragon's mouth – it is his primary tool of intimidation. Don't worry – it's only hot air!

Never address Satan personally – don't talk to him!

Another warning: Avoid becoming preoccupied with Satan and his domain. Have you ever wondered why people are intrigued with movies, video games, and music based on the dark side? One of the games that the enemy plays is creating an unhealthy fascination with his work. Many people are caught up in giving more attention and credit to the enemy than they do God. I call this a "demon behind every bush" mentality. It is common for those struggling with satanic affliction to be preoccupied with the enemy due to their level of temptation, obsession, and negative thoughts. However, one must take special caution to keep their eyes upon Jesus. Well-trained Christians in the Word and Spirit will not fear Satan or his schemes.

The Christian is engaged in a spiritual battle, even if he/she ignores the reality thereof. Satan and his spiritual forces are on the battle line waiting for us each day. A believer does not choose his engagement in this battle, it awaits him each day, and there is no way to get around it. If you are saved and have received Jesus Christ as your Lord and Savior, you are in! Be alert and sober, for your enemy; Satan roams around on the earth to seek whom he can devour. Are you battle-ready? If not, that's OK. This Book of Prayers will equip and ready you for taking on the challenges he and his demonic influence have to offer.

Believers are being awakened to the reality that their fight in life is not against flesh and blood but the powers of darkness and the principalities of the air (see Eph. 6:12). So many Christians today are deceived into thinking that what they see is what they are to battle. As the Lord draws near, we can be assured that our battle with the world, the flesh, and the devil will intensify. Worldly ideas of pop psychology will increase as the primary solution to our troubled minds. More rapidly than most of us realize, the questions people ask are based on worldly fables called philosophies of man.

God is calling each of His children to call upon Him, and He will deliver according to His Divine Truth and Will.

Fear of confronting the enemy has held most believers back from bolding going before the throne of God regarding the temptations and afflictions of the enemy. God's greatest servants have always shared an appreciation of the magnificent power of prayer and the complete victory over Satan's kingdom available to all believers through the mighty Person and work of our Husband, Jesus Christ.

The book of Ephesians is the New Testament handbook on spiritual warfare and prayer. Get to know this book as a handbook. The believer's emphasis in prayer must be upon a biblical and sound doctrinal approach to this subject. The Word of God recognizes that we encounter the three faces of Satan—the world, the flesh, and the devil. When a person becomes born-again, his/her relationship to everything in the physical, spiritual, mental, and the emotional world completely changes. Since the believer is a citizen of heaven, he is given to power to face the enemy toe-to-toe. Scary? Well, look at it this way. Either we face him head-on, or he will constantly be nipping at our heels—eating away our lives a little at a time.

To resist the limited power of the enemy, one must submit to God first, then resist the evil one, and he will flee. It is a promise given to us by God (see James 4:7).

Because of our newfound relationship with God, all believers are marked targets for attack from God's enemy—Satan. Understanding that he is relentless in his attacks, believers must embrace the Truth that the Father has given them a defense system—the power of prayer.

Furthermore, we must not depend upon feelings and experiences as evidence of our being strong enough to pray. The power and ability to pray boldly are based upon objective fact and not upon subjective feelings. The power of prayer is to be appropriated by faith and faith alone. The following are the Five Phases of Effectual Prayers:

1. **Personal Reflection and Confession**
2. **Praise, Thanksgiving, and Adoration**
3. **Alining Oneself with the New Covenant**
4. **Prayers of Supplication**
5. **Worship and Affirmation**

PRAYING ALOUD VS. SILENTLY

The scriptures do not support the ideology of the enemy being able to "read our minds." Silent prayers, prayers prayed in the inner room of our minds, is the safest form of communication with our Savior. Since indwelt believers have the Life and mind of Christ within them (1 Cor. 2:16), private payers coming from the believer's "prayer closet" are mostly honored by our Lord.

*"When you pray, you are **not to be like the hypocrites**; for they love to stand and pray in the synagogues and on the street corners so that they **may be seen by men**. Truly I say to you, they have their reward in full. But you, when you pray, **go into your inner room, close your door and pray to your Father who is in secret**, and your Father who sees what is done in secret will reward*

you. And when you are praying, **do not use meaningless repetition** *as the Gentiles do, for they suppose that they will be heard for their many words. So do not be like them; for your Father knows what you need before you ask Him.* **(Matthew 6:5-8)**

The enemy's goal is to turn all those who pray into hypocrites – Greek meaning, *one who acts on a stage*. Knowing that the enemy has NOT been given the power to read human minds, he must function in temptation externally to recondition the prayer habits of the one praying. He accomplishes this through externally playing on the human's dynamic of fear, the believer's fears associated with *people-pleasing* – who wants to be seen or heard by others. This fulfills his goal of setting the believer's prayer habits in making use of "meaningless repetition." The Greek meaning for "meaningless repetition" is one Word (*battologeo*), meaning, *to stutter, vain requests from obligation*. When people pray from *battologeo*, Satan knows that their prayers have transitioned into a vanity (about self). Vanity is nothing more than performance-based requests, which the Father does not note.

The most honest and earnest requests are typically done in private. Therefore, the Lord tells us to *go into your inner room, close the door and pray to your Father who is in secret*. The Father is not a pleasing public figure. He fully knows the tactics of His enemy (Satan) in public prayers, thus, revealing His method of accomplishing His mighty deeds - through secrecy. The Greek Word being used here for *secret* is *"kruptos,"* which means *concealed, private, hidden, and inward*. It is here we gain insight into the importance of *inward* praying.

When then do we pray aloud, publicly?

The key is for the believer to understand that when prayers go from *inward* to outward, publicly, they understand and are alert to the reality that external manipulation by the enemy is in play.

Remembering, external prayers are not wrong! External prayers are more vulnerable prayers due to exposure to the enemy. External prayers activate the enemy's ability to toss sudden fears into the mix, tempting the prayer warrior to be concerned about what others might think about them and the prayers being offered up.

External prayers are a perfect way to put the enemy in his place – if the prayer warrior is not intimidated, nor moved, by the enemy's tactics.

Public prayers are ideal for showing new believers, or older believers, how to pray publicly – releasing the Spirit to pray through the indwelt believer vs. praying repetitiously, which forms *battologeo* (hypocrisy). After Jesus revealed how to do this, *pray, then, in this way*, we are reminded where His true intercession occurred.

After He had sent the crowds away, He went up on the mountain by Himself to pray; and when it was evening, He was there alone. (Matthew 14:23)

But Jesus Himself would often slip away to the wilderness and pray. (Luke 5:16)

Why was this His primary method and place of prayer? To honor His previous mandate of avoiding the temptations revealed in Matthew 6:5-8. Intercessory prayer also is guarded by the Spirit – blocking the enemy from entering the *inner room.* Whether Jesus prayed aloud in His private place or from the *inner man* is not known to us, NOR does it make any difference due to the protection provided by the Spirit. This same protection applies to all indwelt believers to this day.

Our conclusion is this: the believer's primary venue of prayer should be *in secret.* Our secondary modality of prayer should be publicly (*two or more gathered)*, with the attitude of alertness, guarding oneself against the fears afflicted upon us by the enemy. I believe that public prayers are for the sole purpose of demonstrating the true modality of releasing the Spirit to pray through us and combat the enemy of the external that is oppressing others – via Satan and his demonic beings.

Why am I immovable in this stance?

Jesus Himself said, *for your Father knows what you need before you ask Him* (Matthew 6:8b). This clearly emphasizes the He and not us. When believers pray, they must remember that the Father already knows what they need before they pray. That is why it requires an alinement with the New Covenant, not an appeal, to change the sovereign WILL of God. In this, we find the prerogative to join Him in what is already in play by the Father. Prayer doesn't change God's mind, nor adjust it, to match our rote self-life requests.

Prayer is for reflection, adoration, praise, confession, and aligning ourselves with the preexisting WILL of God. When a believer uses prayer to attempt to change the mind and will of the Father, it puts the petitioner in the seat of the Godhead, manipulating the God of the eternal to adjust His entire plan to match the request of the supplicatory. This will NEVER happen! The only supplications that become "answered prayers" are the prayers that match the preexisting WILL of the Father. All other prayers are disregarded as an attempt to change the eternal to match the self-life requests of the one praying. When the believer supplicates, these supplications need to be with an appeal of realigning their minds with the mind of Christ (1 Cor. 2:16).

PERSONAL REFLECTION AND CONFESSION

The following outline presents a biblical procedure for our personal reflection and confession time with the Lord.

- Engage in an honest appraisal regarding your selfishness. It is important to be open and honest with God about yourself.

- Confess all known sin (1 John 1:9). Verbalize your sins against yourself, others, and God. Don't ask for forgiveness; accept the existing forgiveness He provided through His deeds on the Cross. Confessions take back the ground Satan took from your spiritual walk in Christ.

- Extend forgiveness to those who have hurt you. Unforgiveness is the primary reason most Christians don't pray consistently. List out who hurt you, how they hurt you, and your reactions. Bring the offenders and how they hurt you before Him and extend forgiveness to them in prayer. Now confess to God that your reactions to these offenses are sin, accept His forgiveness, and tell Him you are willing to seek the offenders' forgiveness for those reactions.

- Yield yourself to God (Romans 6:13). As an act of your will (displace your feelings), yield all areas of your life to Him—spiritual, psychological, physical, social, marital, parental, and financial.

- Express your passion and desire for the Holy Spirit to renew your mind.

- Believe with your mind that the Holy Spirit will fill you up with His power—remember to set your "feelings" aside and claim this by faith.

- Now, obey God in all that He reveals and expresses in the Scriptures and begin to pray doctrinally.

Sample Covenant Prayer:

Blessed Holy Father, in the name of my Husband and Savior Jesus Christ, I choose to pray in the Light of the Holy Spirit. I recognize that only as Jesus lives in my life will I be able to escape the works of my flesh. I desire the Holy Spirit to bring all the works of my flesh to death. I choose to bring all the work of co-crucifixion and the resurrection of Christ into my life today. I pray that the life of Christ may produce His fruit within my whole being and fill my heart with Your love for You and others. I claim Your forgiveness for all the ways I have grieved or quenched You. Enable me to embrace and respond to Your grace. Cause me to release Christ's obedience to fulfill Your precious Word. Grant me discernment to resist being deceived by the lies of the enemy. I choose this day to allow the Holy Spirit to control my heart and mind. I apply my Victory in Christ over my flesh and worldly influences. I completely yield my life to You. I now pray that you empower me to bring praise and adoration before your throne. In the name of the Lord Jesus Christ, I receive all the fullness of the Holy Spirit, the fulfillment of the New Covenant into all areas of my being today. Amen.

PRAISE AND ADORATION

Walking after the Spirit is essential if we are to bring praise and adoration before the Father. When God said to enter the courtyard with thanksgiving and prayer—He was quite serious. Many Christians attempt to praise God while having "things" in their lives for which they are not thankful. Philippians 4:6 says, *"Be anxious for nothing, but in everything by prayer and supplication with thanksgiving let your requests be made known to God."* It is difficult, if not impossible, to pray and supplicate with anxiety in our hearts. The way to remove anxious thoughts is through thanksgiving! *"In Him, you also, after listening to the message of truth, the gospel of your salvation—having also believed, you were sealed in Him with the Holy Spirit of promise, who is given as a pledge of our inheritance, with a view to the redemption of God's own possession, to the praise of His glory"* (Ephesians 1:13-14).

Thanksgiving and praise for what He has accomplished for & in us through the Holy Spirit is a great place to start. Once your head is clear, tell Him of your thanksgiving you're your infirmities. Prayers of praise and adoration are simply admiring the Person and work of God no matter you're your "feelings" state or the circumstances you face. It is crucial to acknowledge before God that you are grateful for all things before petitioning your requests.

Sample Prayer of Adoration

Dear Lord, I humbly approach You - the God of Abraham, Isaac, and Jacob - the God of promise, hope, love, and grace. I come before You in the merit, the holiness, and the righteousness of my Husband, the Lord Jesus Christ. I praise You for the blessed ministry of prayer through the Holy Spirit. I thank you for the privilege of intercession for all Your saints.

I praise You for being the God of all the living. I recognize that You are the Life-giver and the substance of my faith. You are the God of perfection and purity. I bless you for the mighty work of the crucifixion, which You accomplished through Jesus. Thank you for the cleansing work you accomplished through the blood of Your Son and for taking the penalty and guilt for my sin. I bless you for the privilege You give me to fellowship with You. Thank You that the work of the Cross brings Satan's work to nothing. I will be grateful all of the days of my life for the deliberate act of the sacrifice You demonstrated by giving Your Only Son to free us from the domain of darkness and transferring us into Your kingdom of light. I will accept any things brought into my life by way of your Sovereign plan. I chose to die to my old ways and count my flesh dead with Christ on the Cross. Therefore, I thank

You for my new identity and praise You for the redemptive act of putting off my old self and granting me new life! I now ask that you receive the prayers of supplication that match Your Holy will. Amen.

ALINEMENT WITH THE NEW COVENANT

This phase of your prayer is the most important. If we don't align thinking with the New Covenant message, our thinking and requests will take the pathway of selfish praying. New Covenant thinking is all about fulfillment versus asking for things – it is more like claiming what is already true about us and the allotment of our daily circumstances. Without this modality of thinking, the enemy will shift our focus from accepting existing sovereignty to begging for God to change His sovereignty to match our panic and fears. Note. He will not change His eternal plan to match humanity's needs. However, since He knows what your needs are before you pray, He will fulfill all the requests that match His predestined care for you.

SAMPLE NEW COVENANT PRAYER

Lord Jesus, I aline myself this day with the work & deliverance you provided on the Cross many years ago. I agree with Your divine fulfillment of meeting all my needs according to Your richness and glory. While I reject the enemy's works, I accept the sovereign will of You, Your Father, and the Holy Spirit. I renounce any temptation to beg You to change Your will to match mine. I ask for a manifestation of the Holy Spirit to accept my human weaknesses and the ramifications it presents. I knowledge that my flesh cannot live life without Your empowerment. I also accept the reality that

Your grace is sufficient AND that Your power is perfected in my weaknesses.

PRAYERS AND SUPPLICATIONS

Intercessory prayer is the practice of praying or applying the objective, absolute Truth of the Word of God as the hope of realigning our will with that of the Father. God loves for us to pray His Word back to Him, claiming His attributes, promises, and redemptive work as the foundation of our faith and hope that He will answer our supplications. Praying His Word is the assurance of praying the will of the Father. However, the hope and solution of the prayer burden are always based upon the objective absolutes of God's attributes and character as revealed in His Holy Word.

Experienced prayer warriors know that using their own ideas or words accomplish nothing, but by using the Word of God in prayers, the enemy (Satan) shutters and backs down. Satan cannot stand when the Word is used to combat the temptations and attacks he presents. Quoting verses while praying is what puts the enemy in his place—dark places. When we attempt to confront the tactics of our foe by using our self-life sincerity and efforts, we will soon discover he is not intimidated. New Covenant praying should occupy much of our daily prayer time. It must be used in praise, petition, and intercession. Herein lies one of God's greatest gifts to us for our prayer time.

Believers have a supernatural resource of wealth and riches in the grace and gifts bestowed upon them in the Lord Jesus

Christ. The Truths are ours for claiming power, position, authority, and total victory over Satan's world, which belongs to God the Father. The believers' victory over the enemy is absolute when he attempts to use God's Truth to defeat us—his primary tactic of deception.

"For though we walk in the flesh, we do not war according to the flesh, for the weapons of our warfare are not of the flesh, but divinely powerful for the destruction of fortresses. We are destroying speculations, and every lofty thing raised up against the knowledge of God, and we are taking every thought captive to the obedience of Christ" (2 Corinthians 10:3-5).

We must learn to pray aggressive warfare prayers for family and friends who struggle with bondage. Pray this prayer aloud when led to intercede for an individual in a public environment.

Sample Prayer of Supplication

My dear heavenly Father, In the name of our Lord Jesus Christ, I bring before You in prayer (loved one's name) _____. I ask for the Holy Spirit's guidance that I might pray in the Spirit as You have taught me. I thank You, Father, that You have sovereign control over _____. I thank You for the spiritual gifs you have placed in _____. In the name of the Lord Jesus and as a priest of God, I ask for mercy and Your invite for them to accept Your forgiveness for the sins by which _____ has grieved You. I plead the sufficiency of the blood of Christ to meet the full penalty their sins deserve. I pray for an opportunity for _____ to claim back the ground they have given to Satan by believing the enemy's deception. In the name of the Lord Jesus Christ, I resist all of

Satan's activity that holds _____ from mercy & deliverance. Exercising my authority which is given to me in my union with the Lord Jesus Christ, I pull down the strongholds which the kingdom of darkness has formed against _____. I smash, break, and destroy all those plans formed against _____'s mind, will, emotions, and body. In prayer, I destroy the spiritual blindness and deafness that Satan keeps on _____. I invite the Holy Spirit of God to bring the fullness of His power to convict, to bring to repentance, and to lead _____ into faith in the Lord Jesus Christ as Savior if not authentically saved. I cover _____ with the blood of the Lord Jesus Christ and ask You to break Satan's power that blinds _____ from seeing the Truth of God.

Believing that You, Holy Spirit, are leading me, I request a deliverance for _____ in the name of the Lord Jesus Christ. If it is Your will to keep _____ in darkness for a while, please release Your patience in those that are praying to accept the Holy timeline of the Living God for the answer to this prayer. In the name of Jesus, I joyfully lay this prayer before You in the worthiness of His completed work. Amen.

Be persistent in praying, Covenant!

It happened that while Jesus was praying in a certain place, after He had finished, one of His disciples said to Him, "Lord, teach us to pray just as John also taught his disciples." And He said to them, "When you pray, say: 'Father, hallowed be Your name. Your kingdom come. 'Give us each day our daily bread. 'And forgive us our sins, For we ourselves also forgive everyone who is indebted to us. And lead us not into temptation.'" Then He said to them, "Suppose one of you has a friend, and goes to him at midnight and says to him, 'Friend, lend me three loaves; for a friend of mine has come to me from a journey, and I have nothing to set before him'; and from inside he answers and says, 'Do not bother me; the door has already been shut, and my children and I are in bed; I cannot get up and give you anything.' "*I tell you, even though he will not get up and give him anything because he is his friend, yet because of his persistence he will get up and give him as much as he needs.* "*So I say to you, ask, and it will be given to you; seek, and you will find; knock, and it will be opened to you.* "*For everyone who asks, receives; and he who seeks finds; and to him who knocks, it will be opened.* "*Now suppose one of you fathers is asked by his son for a fish; he will not give him a snake instead of a fish, will he?* "*Or if he is asked for an egg, he will not give him a scorpion, will he?* "*If you then, being evil, know how to give good gifts to your children, how much more will your heavenly Father give the Holy Spirit to those who ask Him?*" (Luke 11:1-13)

This passage reveals to us three significant things.

The first being that Jesus was praying in a certain place (*private, inner room*) and secondly, the items to include in prayer, and third the method of appealing/aligning oneself with the will of the Father regarding the true needs of the one praying (*get up and give him as much as he needs*). This method of prayer is conclusive and perfect. Pray without ceasing and always be intuitive in and through the mind of Christ to align oneself with the existing will of the Father, who knows what the true needs of His prayer warriors are.

Permissible Suffocation

꒛✝꒜

REFLECTING ON MY LESSONS OF JOB

To derail the temptation for readers to use the "Book of Prayers" as some spiritual formula to deliver them from potentially assigned circumstances of our Lord, I implore you to read this chapter before making use of the prayers and content within this book. The book you are about to read was birthed through the lessons contained within this chapter.

My wife has said for many years, "*I am certain that the older I get – the less I know.*" I cannot tell you how many times those words have rung my bell! I have been a born-again indwelt Christian since I was 16 years of age. I have fought my way through the jungle of deception and worldly fables for over 50 years, and I still ask questions like:

† How could a righteous God allow such an evil world?

† How could a loving God allow the enemy to torture His children with despair and emotional suffocation?

† Why do righteous people suffer when they diligently worked to seek His divine will?

† Why does God allow the ungodly to prosper?

† My utmost favorite is: are adversity and affliction a sign that a suffering Christian have unconfessed sin?

After discipling others in the message of the Exchanged Life (Not I, but Christ: Galatians 2:20) for 30+ years, I have discovered something rather simple but profound. The Exchanged Life, nor expelling doctrinal prayers, rid us of suffering but rather invites it all the more. That leaves us with a question; "Why should we appeal to God to relieve us of sufferings?" That is why I believe this chapter must be read.

MY OWN SUFFERING

Like many (if not most) Christians, I have suffered my measurement of troubles – the type of troubles that bring heartache, physical challenges, and emotional ramifications. The most difficult of all suffering has been the constant unmerciful criticizing from fellow Body members. When fronted with a near-terminal ailment, some Christians dared to conclude that there must be some sin in my life. They pushed and peddled the worldly thought that all suffering is always the result of sin; therefore, simplistically touting that if I (we) repent of this "unknown sin," that the momentary light affliction would somehow disappear. Even though we know the error of this dogmatism, we fall into this dark place of treating repentance like "a pill" – "a pill" that will somehow deliver us from our moments of despair and emotional suffocation.

When is the last time you had a mounting of perpetual circumstances thrown in your face at such a rate that you frequently felt you couldn't surface long enough to take a deep breath? The feeling of suffocation, in my opinion, is one of the worst kinds of suffering. Several years ago, when I first contracted an infection in my heart that ultimately led to heart failure, I had severe problems with my breathing. At first, we thought it was from a head cold. The doctor gave me medication to fight the viral infection. It only made things worst. Next in line was the thought my "childhood asthma" was returning.

Treatment was applied, which of course, made it worse. It was adding to the liquid building up in my lungs. Then it got to the point that I was only able to lay back, forget laying down, for several minutes at a time. Due to only getting minimal sleep a day, they thought I was developing sleep apnea. In reality, I was suffocating. By the time I was admitted to the ER, one lung was filled and the second was at its "half full" mark. I cannot tell you the horrid feelings this suffocation brought on. In fact, at one point in the ER, they were frantically working to "bring me back."

Once arresting the crisis, I was placed in a care unit to begin my healing process. While there, I was visited by an array of "friends" and family. Some visitors came to confess their sins of offense against me, they left, and I never heard from them again. Others came to visit to offer true and respectable comfort. Then, some came as representatives of a "group of friends" to confront me about the "sin" in my life. One "old friend" in particular asked if I thought that God was putting this on me due to some sin in my life.

Now, I am a firm believer in declaring that afflictions sometimes come from God to purify us and that this, in no way, indicates that God is unloving. It is only His way of leading us back to a dependent "talk and walk" relationship to Himself - kind of like a father would discipline a child. Even though I know that suffering instructs us in righteousness and prevents us from sinning, it doesn't make the journey easier. It certainly puts us in the position of determining if we will question God's sovereignty or accuse Him of hurting His children. This all leads to the biggest question of all: *Will we humbly submit ourselves to God's will?*

I don't know about you, but I find God's will at times to be quite painful. I am NOT saying He doesn't provide comfort, healing, and guidance, but I am saying that the walk, for the most part, is at times daunting. To be straightforward, I find that God does not choose to answer most of my penetrating questions. Instead, He overwhelms me with a panoramic view of His creative power and perfect Divine wisdom. I usually get reprimanded for attempting to figure out the reason for my pain and suffering. If you want to talk about sin, this is the sin that gets me in trouble the most. I can't tell you how many times I have walked away from a conversation with God where I felt humbled and a bit foolish for implying that God owes me some type of explanation. Since I will never be big enough to canvas my world, how would I ever presume to tell God how to manage His sovereignty?

I think most indwelt Christians have embraced the fact that Jesus shed His blood to deliver us from our sins, but how many of us have embraced the fullness of His Holy plan? Now, think about it – if we exchange our lives for His, doesn't it mean that in the exchange comes the commission to be willing to share in the sufferings of Jesus?

"Suffer hardship with me, as a good soldier of Christ Jesus."
(2 Timothy 2:3)

"The Spirit Himself testifies with our spirit that we are children of God, and if children, heirs also, heirs of God and fellow heirs with Christ, if indeed we suffer with Him so that we may also be glorified with Him" (Romans 8:16-17).

"For to you it has been granted for Christ's sake, not only to believe in Him, but also to suffer for His sake" (Philippians 1:29).

If you are like most of us fair-weathered Christians, you don't mind the positive attributes of Christ in the great Exchange; but elements that are not so positive, like the "fellowship of His sufferings, well – that is a different story.

"More than that, I count all things to be loss in view of the surpassing value of knowing Christ Jesus my Lord, for whom I have suffered the loss of all things, and count them but rubbish so that I may gain Christ, and may be found in Him, not having a righteousness of my own derived from the Law, but that which is through faith in Christ, the righteousness which comes from God on the basis of faith, that I may know Him and the power of His resurrection and the fellowship of His sufferings, being conformed to His death; in order that I may attain to the resurrection from the dead." (Philippians 3:8-11).

PAIN & SUFFERING – NOT ME

Was there ever a time in your Christian life when you could say that you were righteous in most of your ways while at the same time experiencing little affliction? I have many fond memories of those days…then came God's "permissible affliction." Even though I have wrestled with the "theology" of the purpose of "bad things happening to good people," in my older years, I have come to understand that Satan is the force behind all the calamities that come upon us. Keep in mind that I didn't say "reason," but the "force." I believe this is one of THE most important elements for Christians to understand and believe.

When I prayed the Selfer's Prayer (see APPENDIX section), back in 1979, I thought Exchanging my life for His would minimally reduce my pain and suffering, but little did I expect that it would offer me ALL THE MORE. Right around that same time, in my childlike ignorance, I asked God to grant me half the measurement of wisdom and understanding He gave Solomon, primarily because I "felt" so stupid. After several years of exchanging suffering for more pain, the Lord led me to this passage:

"Because in much wisdom there is much grief, and increasing knowledge results in increasing pain" (Ecclesiastes 1:18).

At first, this passage raised more questions than it answered. From what I have learned from the Holy Scriptures, Satan needs permission from the Father to do his afflictions.

"Now there was a day when the sons of God came to present themselves before the LORD, and Satan also came among them. The LORD said to Satan, 'From where do you come?' Then Satan answered the LORD and said, 'From roaming about on the earth and walking around on it.' The LORD said to Satan, 'Have you considered My servant Job? For there is no one like him on the earth, a blameless and upright man, fearing God and turning away from evil.' Then Satan answered the LORD, 'Does Job fear God for nothing? Have You not made a hedge about him and his house and all that he has, on every side? You have blessed the work of his hands, and his possessions have increased in the land. But put forth Your hand now and touch all that he has; he will surely curse You to Your face.' Then the LORD said to Satan, 'Behold, all that he has is in your power, only do not put forth your hand on him.' So Satan departed from the presence of the LORD" (Job 1:6-12).

There are many theological elements contained within this passage. One that tends to glare at me the most is "permissible affliction." This passage reveals that Satan works to trap and snare God's people, with the deception that it is God's fault and He is "out to get us."

Several other significant doctrinal issues present themselves here. First, we find that Satan had to approach God and get in line with the rest of the "sons of God" – angels. Once Satan was at the bench of God, the two of them had this unique dialogue. God first asked Satan where he came from. It suggested that God didn't know where Satan was or what he was doing. The truth of the matter is that God knew exactly who he was and what he was up to. By proof of most of His dialogues, God reveals the prerogative of being the One who asks the questions – not man or spiritual beings. Next, we see God bringing up the opportunity to persecute Job before Satan could open his mouth to suggest it (v. 8). It's almost like God set the stage of prospering Job to offer Satan this opportunity. Did God desire to bring hurt and destruction upon His beloved servant? Did God have this hidden curiosity to test Job to see if he would be attacked, tempted, drawn into sin, or become trapped by the devil? No – He was confident in the investment He had made in Job up to this point in His Divine design. God knew there was none like Job on the face of the earth. Since God knows and watches every thought and footprint of man, He knew that no man has been able to withstand a full-on attack of Satan since the days of Noah. He had confidence in this!

I believe Satan completely understood the level of character Job radiated. He knew that he couldn't charge Job with any sin because he (Satan) was the author of it. Just as God knew He was confident in Job's obedience to the Word, Satan knew of Job's confidence of disobedience to Satan's words. We have a great standoff between the confidence of God versus the confidence of Satan.

Does Job fear God for nothing?

What is up with this satanic statement of "Does Job fear God for nothing?" (v. 9). The implication here is that Satan thinks Job "fears" God, NOT because of love, but because of the perception that God spoils him with riches, healthy children, and the prosperity assigned. He is under the direct belief that Job would "curse God" and be done with Him if he had these "blessings" or luxuries taken away from him, proving that Job's fear was outward and hypocritical. Satan knows how man's flesh functions – he obeys to get. After all, Satan developed the demonic reward system of "doing to get." The bottom line: Satan was convinced that Job was afraid of being punished by God if he didn't "jump through the hoops" that God set before him.

The second and less primal issue Satan throws God's way is the issue of protection. Satan now tempts God with the twisted truth that Job is righteous because he lives in a bubble, protection, a shield of sorts that God formed around him. The truth of the matter is we can't function righteously without the almighty protection of God, but Satan is hinging Job's life upon this one principle. Yes, God did border Job's life and all that was entrusted to him with angels (hedge) to encamp about him. This passage reveals clear evidence that Satan is a big pouty bully who likes picking on the little guy. He says that if Job didn't have a big brother protecting him, Job would lose the fight. Well, duh! Satan never picks on someone his own size, although a day is coming when he picks a fight with SOMEONE who is truly going to "clean his clock." Typical bully – always thinking he is "the man," all the while suffering with "little man syndrome." Hmm – maybe that is what this is all about.

Allow me to do some immediacy here. Satan believes that Job breaths freely because he is in the protective bubble that God provided for him. Satan suggests having God remove this bubble and allowing him to suffocate Job by way of hellish and demonic circumstances; then, Job is surely to curse God to His face. The second point of immediacy is that Satan knows he can't do a blasted thing without God *"putting forth His hand and touching all that he has."* It is what we call in counseling a covert confession of impotence. Satan NEVER comes out and openly admits he is impotent but manipulates so that a covert confession spills out. This is a classic way of confession for bullies.

The Lord's response to this not so clever form of manipulation, which appeared in Satan's favor, is this. With God saying, *"Behold, all that he has* (externally) *is in your power* (strength), *only do not put forth your hand on him"* (v. 12, parentheses mine), sends him off most assuredly living out his deception. It always amazes me how God will not dialogue, prove, or interact with Satan (or man) over their manipulative and stupid ways. He gives to man, and beast, the appearance of "having their way" for them to learn from the consequences of those ways. What a loving and respectful God we have.

The "Godological" statement here is rather critical for believers to see and embrace. God is not angry and displeased with Job, nor does He want to get some thrill out of hurting him, nor is He gratifying Satan, but He does want Satan to face the doom of his deception once again, while He (God) ultimately enjoys more glory. The truest form of stupidity is picking a fight with someone who has complete control over the universe. This passage shows us how stupid Satan is. Secondly, it shows us that when "bad things" happen to good people, it does not mean that God is angry, disappointed, or "out to get us." God just has a thing about purifying the Bride of Christ for His Son while rubbing Satan's face in his confusion. These are the two primary reasons for the existence of God's creation – to gain a Bride for His beloved Son and provide a place of torment and punishment for Satan. Humans can deluge their minds with other reasons, but these are the simple facts.

"Then the LORD said to Satan, 'Behold, all that he has is in your power, only do not put forth your hand on him.' So Satan departed from the presence of the LORD" (Job 1:12).

With this, the Lord sends a restrained Satan off to accomplish the mission of God, with Satan thinking it is all about his mission. That is the beauty of this story; God proves the stupidity that deception forms when mixed with pride. Satan is nothing but a tool God uses to advance His Kingdom. Why doesn't Satan figure this out? Simply because sin makes him stupid. Satan's limited authority isn't even his – it belongs to God. All authority is owned by the One who imparts it.

"Every person is to be in subjection to the governing authorities. For there is no authority except from God, and those which exist are established by God" (Rom 13:1).

Any human or spiritual being who stretch their imagination to think they have ownership of anything, particularly authority, is suffering from the same deception of Satan himself. Any authority managed is authority assigned. Therefore, God is in sovereign charge of all things, including those who think they are in charge of anything.

The believer's emotions need to be exchanged just like our mind and will. God has blessed us with the positive emotions of Christ Himself; love, joy, cheerfulness, excitement, kindness, peace, and many others. What many of us don't realize is that when we make this great Exchange, we also inherit His emotions: sorrow, grief, misery, moaning, sadness, confusion – for God only knows how long this list is. It is in the back side of humanity's emotions that Satan feeds into. If He, our Lord and Savior, suffered such affliction, then we should also be willing to fellowship in those same sufferings in our Exchange. We should be willing to exchange our sufferings for more of His pain. Ouch – now that is the reality of our exchange that most believers avoid!

I AM A NOBODY

Have you ever had a rapid succession of affliction to the point of not being able to catch your breath between afflictions? This is a classic technique used by the enemy. It is a way of wearing us down to the point of cursing something or someone. This is the technique Satan used on Job and his wife as they were reclining one particular evening. The first wave arrives: the Sabeans attack, and Job loses his oxen, donkeys, and the first group of servants. Then, while the servant delivered this horrid news, wave two came in: a fire broke out and consumed the sheep and servants on another part of their ranch. While listening to the pathetic news of the second servant, wave three arrives: the Chaldeans attack another part of the ranch, take the camels, and kill more servants. Before this servant could finish, the worst news is delivered: Job's sons and daughters were reclining at the eldest brother's house, a great wind came, destroyed the house, and all died – every man, woman, and beast dead - except for Job, his wife, and four messengers (see Job 1:13-19).

Can you imagine the amount of pain and suffering the two of them must have felt? Usually, when one has succession affliction, the overwhelming feeling of suffocation follows. In many cases, it affects breathing. Some faint, some have panic attacks, and others just sink into despair. What did Job do? It says in Job 1:20 that Job shaved his head/beard (a sign of mourning), tore his robe (symbolizing the death of a loved one), fell to the ground, and began worshiping God, saying:

"Naked I came from my mother's womb, and naked I shall return there. The LORD gave, and the LORD has taken away. Blessed be the name of the LORD" (Job 1:21).

Since the day of my Salvation 50 years ago, for the most part, I have embraced affliction as God has allowed it – until these past few years. I am not saying the afflictions He assigned to me throughout my days was easy or lighthearted. But I am saying that I have never experienced this level of suffering - the type of suffering that produced physical, emotional, and spiritual suffocation – the kind that would stretch my Exchanged life with Christ never like before. After being diagnosed with heart failure, my wife wrote in her journal after one of my many moments of permissible suffocation.

I had never seen him in this state in 34 years of knowing him. My earthly "rock" had been broken physically and now soulically (i.e., mind, will, and emotions). Help him, Lord, to embrace your love fully and completely. Let him feel your compassion and kindness. He feels so misunderstood, so kicked in the teeth, so alone, so wanting to die. He is so pessimistic about people's intentions because of hurt. No trust – but suspicious and expectant of betrayal. He has been beaten down by too many for too long, and he is without hope, joy, and strength.

Over the following years since this diagnosis, Job's prayer of desperation and great Exchange has found new meaning in my heart of hearts. Looking back, I came into this world naked, dependent, and very sick – living in an oxygen tent the first five years of my life. I grew up shamed, embarrassed and incompetent in almost everything I said and did. My entire childhood was filled with being hated, despised, and made fun of by family and "friends" - all for the sake of accepting Jesus Christ as my Lord and Savior at 16 years of age. Then shortly after learning to read at the age of 22, God graced me with one of my favorite passages in the Bible:

"Because of the surpassing greatness of the revelations, for this reason, to keep me from exalting myself, there was given me a thorn in the flesh, a messenger of Satan to torment me--to keep me from exalting myself! Concerning this, I implored the Lord three times that it might leave me. And He has said to me, 'My grace is sufficient for you, for power is perfected in weakness.' Most gladly, therefore, I will rather boast about my weaknesses, so that the power of Christ may dwell in me. Therefore I am well content with weaknesses, with insults, with distresses, with persecutions, with difficulties, for Christ's sake; for when I am weak, then I am strong. I have become foolish; you yourselves compelled me. Actually I should have been commended by you, for in no respect was I inferior to the most eminent apostles, even though I am a nobody" (2 Cor. 12:7-11).

Thanks to God, I learned to journal my thoughts in prayer early on. Please keep in mind that these entries are NOT replacing the Word of God – not one bit. They are personal writings of thoughts that I believe God put in my mind to help me understand the Word. Here is what I recorded in my journal shortly after being blessed with this passage:

Stephen, because of your willingness to embrace My Truth and speak it as I reveal it to you, I will be granting you affliction throughout your life for you NOT to exalt yourself. You will often cry out to Me for relief, and I shall grant you comfort, but not necessarily circumstantial deliverance. Stephen, it is through your afflictions and weaknesses that you will discover the power of My grace. As you take this new journey, you will struggle with pride, arrogance, and boasting. I am calling you to boast only in this – that you came into this world weak and dependent, and you will leave it in the same manner. When you were born, you were dependent on man and independent of Me. When you depart from this wicked world, you will be independent of man and completely dependent on Me. When I am finished with you, you will be able to embrace your weaknesses and handle insults, stress, and imparted hatred with the power of Grace. In the end, you will shine for your acute ability to hear Me, understand the deeper Life, and lead others into like-minded Truth – even though in the world's eyes, you will be a nobody. Stephen, do you have ears to listen?

Well – when the Lord revealed this to me, I had no clue as to how much suffering was ahead of me. For 65+ years, my life has been filled with many external hardships. More recently, being diagnosed with CIDP, a neurological disease that destroys my nerve sheaths, causing paralysis. However, I must say the toughest has been the rejection from so-called self-proclaimed "Christians." The portion of the passage that I didn't give a second thought to at the time - became my worst struggle in life.

> *"I have become foolish; you yourselves compelled me. Actually I should have been commended by you, for in no respect was I inferior to the most eminent apostles..."* (2 Cor. 12:11).

I expect the unbelieving world to hate me because of Christ. What surprised me was the level of backstabbing, kissing on the cheek, and rejection from the "body of Christ." For most of my adult Christian life, I fought this and was compellingly confused by it. In my naive way of living out my Christian life, I thought the Body of Christ would be the first to build me up in Christ, patch up my wounds, and send me back into battle. It was a bit shocking to discover this was not the case. This soul-shaking reality was what God used their covert hatred to open the door to my ministry – ministering to a broken church that is neither hot nor cold, but rather lukewarm - the church of Laodicea (the 'Cancel Culture Church'). It became evident that this group of fake Christians were not the authentic Body of Christ. These non-members act like real Christians, but in actuality, they are as fake as a bowl of plastic fruit, who cannot love me or any other Body member with the authentic Love of God. God uses their rejection to rid me of pride and assist me in a deeper dependence on the indwelling Life of Jesus.

I have come to realize that the power of the Cross has a significant impact on my emotions. The hard and sobering lesson here for me is that after the Cross made this impact, Christ's life in me expects the emotions to no longer be an obstruction, but rather to be cooperative with the Spirit of Life that indwells my mortal body – to embrace the full exchange. You see, the fact that I died with Christ on His Cross gives me the freedom to claim the death of my emotional reactions as to why I am hanging on it. Once I can experientially digest this, then my emotions can be renewed along with my mind and thus, provide a pathway for the Spirit to express the emotions of Christ through me.

THE ELEMENTS OF PAIN

When we commit ourselves to the power of the Cross, we must remember that this commitment does not free us from the "fellowship of His sufferings." The old self and its function were nailed to the Cross with Christ and our crucifixion with Him. This was not to stop us from thinking, choosing, or feeling. On the contrary – it was for us to think, choose, and feel righteous. The Cross ends the nasty flesh bondage that typically leads us to giving the enemy, Satan, too much credit.

My mind tends to look at details that frequently don't stand out on the page. An example is the passage of permissible affliction in Job 1:13-19, which few of us take the time to review. Who does Satan use to do this affliction? What techniques does he use? What elements of permissible power does he have? In asking these questions of myself, I found something rather interesting. In my discovery, I found three primary forms of attack or permissible affliction that God uses to assist us in a true exchange of life.

The first form of permissible affliction is his use of humans who have partnered in the enemy's deceptive ways. Look at the Sabeans in verse 15. The Sabeans were descendants of the cursed lineage of Ham. They were haters of the God of Abraham and all of His children. Then we have the Chaldeans in verse 17 – they were the Babylonians. Babylonia was the nation that birthed some of the evilest nations in the world. What are the Chaldeans most known for?

"For behold, I am raising up the Chaldeans, that fierce and impetuous people who march throughout the earth to seize dwelling places which are not theirs" (Hab. 1:6).

Here we have Satan being granted permission to afflict Job. He accomplishes his mission through willing earthlings who seem to be pons of possession. I have come to realize that there is really nothing new under the sun in my older age. Satan's approach to slowing the righteous people has not changed all that much. He still uses "fake" followers to sneak in the back door to deliver despair and hopelessness.

The second element of permissible affliction granted to Satan seems to be the elements – earth, wind, and fire (v. 16). No, not the rock band, but the band of rocks that are about to fall in on Job's family. Even though God ultimately controls the elements, permission is granted. I see this as the enemy toying with our externals, delivering destruction to form unrest, inconvenience, or financial hardship. He knows that our flesh tends to find security in the things we can see. Since he is a god of the externals, he also knows that if he keeps the externals unpredictable and constantly changing, eventually, it will bring predictable despair.

The third and final element is physiological health. Job's response of falling on the ground and worshipping God was not an expected one. After taking away all of his externals (except for his wife), Satan proved God to be right. We are not sure how much time passed between the first appeal to God and the second one. Many Jewish writers have believed it to be one year. This is not likely, as Satan would never give him so much breathing time; nor can it be thought that Job's friends would stay away so long before they paid him a visit, which was not until after the second appeal. In any case, we find him at the Lord's workbench again. The same question is put to him by God, and the same answer is given. Interestingly enough, God suggests another attack on Job. God cites the same verbiage regarding Job's integrity, but this time He adds, *"And he still holds fast his integrity, although you incited Me against him, to ruin him without cause"* (Job 2:3). With that, Satan becomes a bit more belligerent – *"Skin for skin! Yes, all* *that a man has he will give for his life (skin). However, put forth Thy hand, now, and touch his bone and his flesh; he will curse Thee to Thy face"* (Job 2:4-5, parentheses added).

You would think that Satan would have seen the proof of Job's integrity by now. But he still believes Job was a selfish and mercenary type; what had been done to him was not a sufficient enough trial to truly test his integrity, and the affliction had not been intense enough to discover the real man. I believe this reveals Satan's belief that a man can lose all his externals, but as long as he enjoys physical health – it will be easy for him to serve God. The general sense of the passage here is plain, for the enemy is proclaiming that a man would give everything he had to save his hide (skin). I think Satan believes that Job is so afflicted in his body that he likely wants to die, or at least give up his faith in God, to save his hide.

Despite the deception Satan is under, God puts Job back into his hands once again. God allows full-on attack but will not allow the enemy to take Job's breath from him. Personally, after studying the book of Job – death would have been a welcomed option.

Job is about to be tested beyond human strength and willpower. He is about to learn what the backbone of the Exchanged Life is. Just because Job walked uprightly and unexceptionally to the will of God does not necessarily guarantee him to have made the true Exchange – Not I, but God.

It is an impossible feat to try to separate the power of the Cross from the power given to us through the Resurrection.

"For if we have become united with Him in the likeness of His death, certainly we shall also be in the likeness of His resurrection" (Romans 6:5).

As Job learned, the death we experience on the Cross with Christ does not give us a way of escape from the pain of the Cross, but rather a way to bear with it. Every time I watch movies or media clips that depict our Lord bearing the pain resulting from our sins, I weep like a child. Even though I know there are two types of suffering, consequences for my sins and, secondly, for the sins of others, I still find myself caught in the snag of refusing to suffer. Humm – maybe God wants me to have a proper perspective of 'hate.'

"He who loves his life loses it, and he who hates his life in this world will keep it to life eternal" (John 12:25)

SATAN USED BY GOD TO BREAK US

There is an adage that says, *"The thing that holds our affections holds our souls."* Whether it was the Chinese, the Christians, or the Chaldeans who gave us this proverb, they were right on. The baptism of fire that our Lord speaks of is to quickly "burn off" all people, places, and things that hold our affections outside of the will of God. The Lord is pretty single-minded about where our affections should be lodged. Anyone, who has placed his affections in anything else besides God, is challenging God to put a permission slip in the hand of his enemy (Satan) to refine him and purify his intentions of affection.

As in the Biblical account of Job, we see Satan is given a permission slip by God to sift and afflict Job. The enemy has been given the power to afflict Job in any manner, including disease, providing the affliction is not terminally fatal. What does he pick? Suspected leprosy, a disease involving nerve infection, boils, and ulcerated sores, is considered one of the most painful disorders known to man. If you have ever had a single boil (sore), you know how painful it can be. If you have ever had an infected boil, you know how quickly it can spread. Now try to imagine about 150 of those spread throughout your entire body – primarily to the feet, buttocks, face, and hands. Job had these ulcers from the soles of his feet to the top of his head. Chapter 2:8 shows us this:

"And he took a potsherd to scrape himself while he was sitting among the ashes" (Job 2:8).

Potsherd was a fragment of broken pottery – a homemade knife. The object was for the sole purpose of removing the filth of accumulated infection that was layering upon each festering sore. Sitting among the ashes was a practice of forced humility and confession to the greatness of one's calamity and sorrow. Back during the ancients of days, people were accustomed to showing their grief by significant external actions, like sitting in ashes. It represented death (from dust to dust and ashes to ashes). Nothing could more strongly express the humility that comes with calamity. Here was a man of wealth, honor, and distinction sitting down in a pile of ashes, taking pieces of broken pottery and scraping the oozing infected sores that covered his naked body. It does not appear anything was done to bring relief or healing, nor any kindness shown in taking care of his disease – not even from his wife.

Here sat a man in a pile of ashes who was once sought after. Now, it would seem, he was completely separated and rejected by all - even those who claimed to "love" him. He was now a diseased man, whom none would venture to approach, and was doomed to endure his suffering without sympathy from others. I'm not sure which is worse - his physical pain or the sorrow of being completely alone. No children, grandchildren, servants, friends, or even a committed and loving wife. Speaking of Job's wife, what was up with her?

"Then his wife said to him, 'Do you still hold fast your integrity? Curse God and die!'" (Job 2:9).

Job's wife was no ordinary woman; she was the blood of Jacob. Her name is unknown. But in ancient versions of this passage, the English word for wife, in Hebrew, is *diynah* (daughter of Jacob). Can you imagine the sorrow she was experiencing? Day after day, she watched her husband suffer, all while attempting to process her grief: the disappearance of her earthly securities, the loss of ten sons and daughters, the heartache and sorrows of her womb, and most likely thinking that she had toiled laboriously in vain. Now she watched her beloved sitting among loathsome worms and ashes, passing the night in the open air, cutting on himself with earthenware, watching the sun go down upon his sorrows day after day, without any sudden relief from their God. I, too, would be tempted to be done with it all. I understand the spotlight was on Job, but Job's wife shares his sorrow. Even though our women carry our sorrow for us in ways that are incomprehensible to us as men, it was the *"curse God"* portion of her speech that aroused the rebuke of her husband.

"But he said to her, 'You speak as one of the foolish women speaks. Shall we indeed accept good from God and not accept adversity?' In all this Job did not sin with his lips" (Job 2:10).

This tells me that Job's wife was a good woman filled with wisdom and truth. She was not a foolish nagging woman of her time. Her sorrow was overtaking her, and she wanted relief. Seriously, who would blame her? I have a woman like this who is faithful as the day is long. But mess with her husband, and you'll hear about it. As with Job's wife, she deeply carries the sorrow of her husband, children, and grandchildren. She, too, has had her moments of giving up. I, like Job, have been blessed with one of the daughters of Jacob. She is frequently the breath within my being when I have enough breath barely to breathe. So, I think I understand why Satan was not allowed to touch Job's wife. God needed her to be the completer of Job during his great sorrow and use her womb to bless Job with seven more sons and three daughters. One of my favorite Scriptures in the Bible is: *"And in all the land no women were found so fair as Job's daughters..."* (Job 42:15). I prayed this Scripture over each of my baby girls as God brought them into this world. You might have guessed; I have a ton of respect for Job's wife. I have wept over her sorrow many times.

Now, Job's "friends" are a different story. I call them his "fair-weather" fellows. These friends got the news their faithful and "beloved friend" was under some severe suffering. The first challenge was that wealthy men tend to speak through their wealth, which is exactly what took place in their dialogue with Job. No matter what is said about those with excessive money, wealth does tend to camouflage sorrow. When counsel is passed through earthly securities, it tends to turn lukewarm or emergent rather quickly. Job certainly learned this.

DON'T BANK ON THE COMFORT OF "FRIENDS"

Why did Job's comforters decide to come? The Scriptures tell us their initial intention was to "sympathize" and "comfort" him. I guess the question would be what the definition of comfort was to these so-called "friends'? Comfort means so many different things to so many people. To some, it is using pain to confront, while with the authentic, it is putting your feet in the fire with the one suffering. For wealthy people, hardship is typically a result of missing the reward. They're inclined to believe something (sin) is stopping the flow of prosperity. They also tend to live based on the reward system: you do well, you get "good things"; you do badly, "bad things happen to you." These men came to comfort a barely recognizable man due to his disfiguring disease, and in such pain, no words could bring comfort.

"When they lifted up their eyes at a distance and did not recognize him, they raised their voices and wept. And each of them tore his robe and they threw dust over their heads toward the sky. Then they sat down on the ground with him for seven days and seven nights with no one speaking a word to him, for they saw that his pain was very great" (Job 2:12-13).

Friend One: I look back on my heart failure hospital experience at several visitors who had come to bring me comfort. While I was fighting for my life, the first was a young man who came to clear his conscience. He said, "I couldn't bear the thought of something happening to you (death) before I got a chance to seek your forgiveness." I smiled, he confessed more stuff, we prayed, and I never saw or heard from him again. To whom was he comforting? Was it me? Not really. In due time, I looked back at this as an enormous act of betrayal. For him, it was an obvious act of freeing himself from a life of guilt.

Friend Two: Another visitor came with yet another form of comfort. This one was from the land of wealth. After a period of silence, he asked, "Do you think there is something in your life that would cause God to allow this?" After I told him my heart failure resulted from a virus and that I didn't want God to let up on this sovereignty act until I learned everything He had in store for me. A look of disappointment came over his face. It was as if he wanted me to suffer under the condition of "God's rebuke." Through this particular "friend's" expression of comfort, it appeared his punishment of me was cloaked in the misnomer of "friendship."

Friend Three: There was yet another kind of comforter who came to see me that week; those who feared what would happen to them if their "counselor" was dead. These "friends" came with words and gifts of comfort. But within a short period, the discussion turned toward their problems. While I am functioning on 11% heart function, on a heart transplant list, gasping for breath, they started asking for counsel without delay. This group opened my eyes to yet another reality of true friendship. As in the case of Jesus's disciples being asleep in the Garden as He suffered, I realized that the true friend is the One who lives inside the one who is suffering – Jesus.

Four different types of friends came to visit me that week, but the third was the most difficult to embrace. The first group: well, one can't expect depth out of shallowness. The second group: I could appreciate his desire for freedom. But, the third: these people thought they were true and honorable friends. They were fearful of what the cost would be like for them if I weren't around. They suffered from the deception that they were close friends because they were close enough to get regular counsel. The problem was - I was caught up in the deception as well. I had to be shown by the Lord that I, too, found closeness and friendship in giving my life away. My grievous struggle came when group three took a hike. Yes. Full-on betrayal. When they discovered that I was not available for "regular" counsel, they were nowhere to be found. Sparse spiritual, psychological, or physical support was offered. One of my board members said in one of our moments of deep emotional need, *"Now is the time when you will discover who your real friends are."* After this experience, I hate to admit it, but I am a man of many acquaintances but few friends.

The fourth group of friends is who God used to sustain me & my family in the most difficult year of my life. These friends remain steadfast in our lives to this day. But, honestly stating, it was the first three groups that God shared some very intimate lessons.

Much can be learned about a man by his confession. What words come out of the mouth when pain and suffering finally break him? Does he curse God? Man? Both? Or do his words level the playing field of his existence? One of the critical points of interest I have learned to watch for in myself and others is: To whom and where does the blame get cast? Can Christians who have not experienced the Exchanged Life truly provide Christ as Life comfort and compassion? All these questions are reasonable questions begging for great answers. In the up-and-coming chapters, you will discover the kinds of prayers the Lord birthed through my suffering, as well as through the sufferings of others.

ENGAGING OUR SUFFERINGS

Have you ever been in a position where you had to sit through a sharing time with a "friend" who truly thought their counsel was perfect for you, and in reality, you knew by the standards of God they were missing the point completely? For those of you who have, you know it isn't any fun.

If we count on the words of others, we miss out on the Word of God. God wants us to embrace that all things come by the permissible Hand of the Almighty. I agree that most Christians suffer from embracing the "why" God allows suffering. Honestly, it is a God thing, not a human thing. Figuring out the "why" is usually what gets us into trouble with the Lord. The key is not understanding the "why," it is in accepting the "why not."

"But it is still my consolation, and I rejoice in unsparing pain, that I have not denied the words of the Holy One." (Job 6:10 NASB)

In reflecting on my notes with my study of Job – I learn that he is careful not to curse God in his words or conclusions. He is in great wonder as to why he should be waiting for the answer to his cry. He wants to know the end reason for his waiting so he can endure with confidence. He certainly has a small confidence problem but not the kind that accuses the mind of the Lord. As for his friends, he asks: For the despairing man there should be kindness from his friend; so that he does not forsake the fear of the Almighty. Job is not getting a lot of compassion from his first "friend." He even goes so far as to say that his *brothers have acted deceitfully like a wadi (brook), as the torrents of wadis which vanish, which are turbid because of ice and into which the snow melts*. In other words, here today and gone tomorrow, they are not providing him with any proper counsel that will empower him to keep up the good fight. The truth of the matter is that these "friends" came in confounded and perplexed – they have no clue how to comfort their "brother." These "friends" see the terror striking the life of Job, and they too are afraid; Job says, *you see terror and are afraid*.

Job doesn't want anything from these men, outside of a little empathy and comfort. He isn't even asking for them to deliver him from the hand of adversity or redeem him from the hand of tyrants. Job does humble himself by saying: *Teach me, and I will be silent; and show me how I have erred*. He goes on to say: *how painful are honest words but what does your argument prove*? He even goes so far as asking them to *please look at me, and see if I lie to your face*. Since they are incapable of offering such solace, Job's discomfort deepens. Due to this, Job asks his "friends" to *desist now, let there be no injustice; even desist, my righteousness is yet in it*. Through all of this, Job still is about his wits. There is no injustice on his tongue, and he continues to be able to discern calamity!

I think maybe the pain that Job suffered at the hand of his "friends" foolish counsel was equally or more painful than his state of ashes. Suffering without receiving help and guidance from a counselor is the worst kind of suffering there is. When you hurt as bad as Job did, every breath you take begs for redemptive freedom. When you are begging to have, someone help you embrace your pain but instead, you are told to "work harder" and "stop whining," well reader – that would be like asking for a drink of water and getting a sponge full of vinegar instead. Sound familiar?

DEFENDING YOUR SUFFERING

I have been professionally counseling for well over 40 years, and I cannot remember one counselee that was not quick to defend their suffering. Some lie and flat out make up wild reasons for their pain and suffering, while others beat themselves to an emotional death before another has the opportunity to do so. In all cases and both extremes, self-pity rules man's flesh even while he/she is searching to discover the reason for it. Reader, this is normal for all of us when walking AFTER our flesh.

A child of God can't understand the Exchanged Life without embracing the privilege and reason for the pain God has granted them to suffer. Often when a person does not discover the reason for their pain – suicide is sure to follow, either emotionally or physically.

Mankind has fallen far from Him, for they call upon the deception of power, fame, and a name they try to make for themselves. When man exalts his name above the Lord's, they deny the power of His name.

God's perspective of my despair is not focused on me, but rather on Him accomplishing His work through me! And if you notice, it is not the work He does IN Me, that's a given, but rather the work He does THROUGH me – that is what matters.

Here we see the difference between He and me. God is all about Himself. He is the only One who has the right to be "self-centered" – rightfully so. I wonder if this was a full-on lesson God was showing Job. Even though we know that the real issue of the story of Job is all about God and His adversary Satan, but my experience is that God makes use of everything Satan throws at His people. God wants Job to proclaim and declare that there is NO God like his God. He wants him to recount the order since the birth of Job's life – which he (Job) is presently cursing. He wanted Job to declare to the world the things that are coming and the events that will occur once this trial is behind him. He certainly did not want Job to forget the promises He gave him throughout his life. God had a specific purpose for Job's life, and it appears that Job struggled in losing sight of it.

Who is like God? Seriously! We should be proclaiming and declaring it; yes, recounting it to Him in order, from the time that He established His calling for our lives. Declare to the world the things that are coming and the events that are going to take place. As God has sent us out, He does not want us to be afraid and tremble but rather announce the victories of Christ. We should never forget the promises He has given us in our youth regarding speaking out His message for all to hear. We must quit using the excuse that we are untrained or youthful and simply go forth and proclaim His Words.

This is why I have such a respect for Job. His level of suffering did not stop him from speaking the truth - even during His worst moments of suffocation. He was truly a man of the Exchanged Life and full of wisdom. His life story reminded me of some very powerful words of Jesus in Luke:

From everyone who has been given much, much will be required; and to whom they entrusted much, of him they will ask all the more. (Luke 12:48)

Could this be what is going on between God and our suffering? Is our level of suffering comparable to our level of wisdom and knowledge? I say – yes!

Because in much wisdom there is much grief, and increasing knowledge results in increasing pain. (Ecclesiastes 1:18)

As you make use of **The Book of Prayers** as a resource in daily living, please allow the Spirit to bring remembrance the words of Romans:

In the same way the Spirit also helps our weakness; for we do not know how to pray as we should, but the Spirit Himself intercedes for us with groanings too deep for words; and He who searches the hearts knows what the mind of the Spirit is, because He intercedes for the saints according to the will of God. And we know that God causes all things to work together for good to those who love God, to those who are called according to His purpose. (Romans 8:26-28)

GENERAL WARFARE

Selfer's Prayer

ଚ✝ଚ

"But if, while seeking to be justified in Christ, we ourselves have also been found sinners, is Christ then a minister of sin? May it never be! "For if I rebuild what I have once destroyed, I prove myself to be a transgressor. "For through the Law I died to the Law, so that I might live to God. "I have been crucified with Christ; and it is no longer I who live, but Christ lives in me; and the life which I now live in the flesh I live by faith in the Son of God, who loved me and gave Himself up for me.
(Galatians 2:17-20)

ENCOURAGEMENT:: Because the objective of an Exchanged Life believer is to become victorious, indwelt Christians and ministers of the Cross, we should not aim merely at helping ourselves or others at resolving "problems." Most people perceive as problems may be God's instruments for accomplishing the most significant work in an indwelt believer – that of being brought to the end of oneself. Without those "impossible situations," we might never have come to the place of brokenness and emptiness before our Groom and Savior, and through this "death" entered into Christ's resurrection power and life as a daily reality.

There is a nasty habit in the church today of thinking that counseling is the answer to all "psychological" issues in a person's life. This is a fantasy resulting from a church that referred people away from the church when "counseling was needed." The irony of this twist is that God works diligently to send hurting souls to the church, while 91% of American churches refer people away from the church when the hurting soul reveals "counseling related" issues that are beyond prayer or Bible reading! In reality, God has empowered every believer with the indwelling power of the Holy Spirit to offer wise counsel and assist others in repentance in wrong attitudes and actions (sin). It is the experience of most Exchanged Life workers that when the Holy Spirit is released to be obedient to Christ within the worker – transformation is quick and certain. And when I was getting my Master's degree, it was stated that the average stay of counseling is 10—12 years. There seems to be something wrong with that picture.

Anyone who has worked with a hurting soul knows that the process is dirty and messy, and it is due to this mess the discipler needs the mind of Jesus to do the work through them. This requires the believer to self-reckoned oneself to be dead, and this must start with a prayer – the Selfer's Prayer. This way, we will not be so apt to function like a "texted-book" Christian, doing to get. If we focus on being a Christ as Life believer, we will be more apt to invest our own lives in another so that Christ will be formed in the one being ministered to. This certainly means that we need to start at the foot of the Cross. Considering praying the following prayer.

PRAYER

I, at this moment, surrender everything that I am, and have, and ever will attempt to be. I take my hands off of my life and release every relationship to You: every habit, every goal, my health, my wealth, and everything that means anything. I surrender it ALL to You. By faith, I take my place at the Cross, believing that when the Lord Jesus was crucified, according to Your Word, I was crucified with Him; when He was buried, I was buried; when He was raised from the dead, I was raised with Him. I deny myself the right to rule and reign in my own life, and I take up the Cross believing that I was raised from the dead and seated at Your right hand.

I thank You for saving me from my sins and myself. From this moment on, I am trusting You to live Your life in me and through me, instead of me; to do what I can't do; quit what I can't quit; start what I can't start; and--most of all--to be what I can't be. I am trusting you to renew my mind and heal damaged emotions in Your time. I thank You now by faith for accepting me in the Lord Jesus, for giving me Your grace, Your freedom, Your joy, Your victory, and Your righteousness as my inheritance. Even if I don't feel anything, I know that Your Word is true; I am counting on Your Spirit to do what Your Word says-- to set me free from myself, that Your resurrection life may be lived out through me, and that You may receive all the glory.

I thank You and praise You for victory right now in Jesus' name, Amen.

Victory

☙✝❧

*"But thanks be to God,
who gives us the victory through our Lord Jesus Christ."*
(1 Corinthians 15:57)

PRAYER

Dear Abba Father, I lift Your holy name in the name of Jesus Christ, my Lord. I praise You that Satan is a defeated enemy. I take great joy in the fact that Jesus accomplished Satan's defeat by giving up His life on the Cross. I appropriate Jesus' death, burial, resurrection, and ascension in my daily living. I look forward to the day that Satan is bound to the bottomless pit for eternity. I rejoice that You, the King of kings and Lord of lords, give me perfect unity and victory over the enemy today.

I choose to enter into my victory and claim my place as being more than a conqueror through Christ who loves me. I refuse to admit to ongoing defeat by Satan in any area of my life. He cannot and will not rule over me, my family, or any of my loved ones. I affirm that Your grace and mercy rule all areas of my life through my union and victory in Christ. Please give me the strength and grace to affirm Your Truth in times of temptation. I bless and thank You for these daily battles and that You seek to accomplish Your divine will in my life. I accept the battlefield You have placed me in today and rejoice in Your divine purpose of it. I reject all of the satanic purposes the enemy has hidden behind his attacks. Through the victory of my Warrior and Savior, I stand resolute and strong upon the certainty of my victory. In confidence, I commit to coming before Your throne boldly each day. All this I do in the name and authority of the Lord Jesus Christ. **Amen.**

Protection

❧✝☙

For wisdom is protection just as money is protection, but the advantage of knowledge is that wisdom preserves the lives of its possessors.
(Ecclesiastes 7:12)

PRAYER

Dear Heavenly Father, I come before You boldly on behalf of _____. I cover _____ with the blood of the Lord Jesus Christ as protection during this time of prayer. I surrender _____ to You completely and unreservedly in every area of their life. I take a stand against all of the workings of Satan that would hinder _____ from this time of prayer. I commit the two of us to the true and living God and refuse any involvement of Satan in our prayer.

Lord, we thank you for keeping the enemy away during our time of prayer. We confirm the blood of the Lord Jesus Christ during our prayer time.

I pray that You Lord Jesus, blessed Holy Spirit, would bring all the work of the crucifixion, all the work of the resurrection, all the work of the glorification, and all the work of Pentecost into _____'s life today. I surrender _____ to You. I renounce all discouragement, guilt, and condemnation from being in _____'s heart and mind. I pray now that You would release _____ to pray this prayer of repentance.

You, Lord, have proven Your power by resurrecting Jesus Christ from the dead. I claim in every way Your victory over all satanic forces active in his life, and I reject these forces. I pray in the name of the Lord Jesus Christ with thanksgiving. In Jesus' name, you, _____ are now released to pray! In Jesus' name, I pray. **Amen.**

Repentance

❧✝☙

"When they heard this, they quieted down and glorified God, saying, "Well then, God has granted to the Gentiles also the repentance that leads to life."
(Acts 11:18)

PRAYER

Heavenly Father, I praise Your name for the grace that has come to me through the Lord Jesus Christ. I rejoice in the victory, which You have provided for me to live above sin and failure. I come before You in confession and to plead Your mercy over my own sins. I confess my sins of lukewarmness, apathy, and worldliness. I specifically confess my sin of _____ (list all the known sins that have bound you – adultery, drug abuse etc.). I acknowledge before You the wickedness of the worldly environment by which I have allowed myself to be influenced. I accept Your forgiveness and mercy for these sins. I plead the sufficiency of the blood of Christ to meet the full penalty of what my sins deserve. I claim back the ground in my life, which I have given over to Satan by believing the enemy's deception. In the name of the Lord Jesus Christ, I resist all of Satan's activity that is holding me blind and causing me to function in darkness. Exercising the authority of Christ, which is given to me in my union with the Lord Jesus Christ, I pull down the strongholds, which the kingdom of darkness has formed against me. I smash, break, and destroy all those plans formed against my mind, will, emotions, and body. In prayer, I destroy the spiritual blindness and deafness that Satan has kept upon me. I invite the Holy Spirit of God to bring the fullness of His power to convict, to bring me to further repentance, and to lead me into faith in the Lord Jesus Christ. I claim the Truth that Satan has no power to blind me from Your Truth.

I thank You for bringing me under conviction, leading me to pray this prayer of repentance, and for answering my prayer of deliverance. I joyfully lay this prayer before You in the worthiness of Christ and the completed work on the Cross. In the name of the Lord Jesus Christ, Amen.

Mental Protection

֎†֍

"Take the helmet of salvation"
(Ephesians 6:17a,)

"And do not be conformed to this world, but be transformed by the renewing of your mind, so that you may prove what the will of God is, that which is good and acceptable and perfect."
(Romans 12:2)

PRAYER

Loving Heavenly Father, I take by faith the helmet of Salvation. I recognize that my Salvation is in the Person of Your Son, Jesus Christ. I cover my mind with His. I desire that He put His mind within me. Let my thoughts be His thoughts. I open my mind fully and only to the control of the Lord Jesus Christ. Replace my own selfish and sinful thoughts with His. I reject every projected thought of Satan and his demons; I, instead, request the mind of Christ. Grant me the wisdom to discern thoughts from the world, my old sin nature, and Satan's kingdom.

I praise You, Heavenly Father, that I may know the mind of Christ as I hide Your Word within my heart and mind. Open my heart to love Your Word. Grant to me the ability and capacity to understand large portions of it. May Your Word be over my mind like a helmet of strength, which Satan's projected thoughts cannot penetrate. I accept Your forgiveness for my neglect and failure to aggressively take the Salvation always available to me. Cause me to fulfill the discipline of daily duty to appropriate Your Salvation. These things I lay before You in the precious name of my Savior, the Lord Jesus Christ. **Amen.**

Forgiving Others

❦✝❧

"Sufficient for such a one is this punishment which was inflicted by the majority so that on the contrary you should rather forgive and comfort him, otherwise such a one might be overwhelmed by excessive sorrow."
(2 Corinthians 2:6-7)

ENCOURAGEMENT: While all sins deserve punishment, this passage is the restoration process of the man Paul had removed from the church. It had accomplished all that Paul had desired; by humbling and bringing to repentance the man living in open sin. As that had been done, it was proper now that this man should be again restored to the privileges of the church. No evil would result from such a restoration, and the church's duty to their penitent brother demanded it. Paul handles the subject here with very great tenderness and delicacy. The entire passage relates solely to this offending brother, yet Paul never once: mentions his name or his crime, any descriptive words that would be calculated to wound this man's feelings, transmit his name to a future generation, nor communicate his name in a harmful way to other churches. Paul speaks of him only in the soft terms of "such a one" and "anyone." How different this is from the temper of those who would try to defame or gossip about the names of offenders or make a permanent record to bring them down with dishonor. Paul is demonstrating the fullness of forgiveness – discipline, forgiving, and restoration. I think that is the point of forgiveness. This prayer is critical and truly a centerpiece of God's divine forgiveness and restoration.

PRAYER

Lord Jesus, Heavenly Father, I have sinned against You and _____ (person to whom you are embittered) by harboring resentment, hurt, and bitterness for their offense against me. I apply Your forgiveness and cleansing of these sins. I now unconditionally forgive _____ for the wrong committed against me. I ask that You would reclaim all ground in my life that Satan's kingdom has claimed against me because of my unforgiveness and bitterness. In the name of Jesus and the power of the Holy Spirit, I stand against any lies and powers of darkness that were assigned against me because of my unforgiving ways. I submit myself to You and ask that You turn me into a vessel of forgiveness.

I choose now to love _____ with Your love, acceptance, and forgiveness. I offer myself up to You as a living sacrifice to be used by You to rebuild the relationship if You deem it necessary. I pray that You would empower me with the strength I need to go to _____ and seek their forgiveness for my part of the offense or my reactions. I ask that You would cover me with the power of Your grace and mercy. It is in the Forgiver's name (Jesus Christ) I pray. **Amen.**

How to Extend Forgiveness

୨୦✝ଓ

Purpose Statement

Offering forgiveness to those that hurt you, in and through Christ, is one of the most freeing actions you can demonstrate here on earth. This homework assignment will include listing the act, your hurt, the ramifications, and your sinful reactions to how the offender hurt you. Once you have done this, you will need to depend upon the eternal forgiver that lives and indwells you – Christ. If you are not a Christian (never have asked Christ into your life), these actions will be temporary and not eternal.

Offering Forgiveness Is Not . . .

It is not "acting" as if it does not bother you anymore. It is not disregarding, tolerating, excusing, overlooking, or closing your eyes to the wrong another person has done against you. It is not "letting time pass" after the offense has been committed. It is not "forgetting" that the offense happened – or "pretending" that it did not happen. It is not "resigning" yourself to the other person's actions by saying, "Oh well, that's just the way he/she is."

Key Statement:
Forgiveness is functioning with another as if they never committed the offense in the first place. Without true forgiveness, you will stay resentful, lack in joy, and act offended any time you see, hear of or meet someone who reminds you of this offender.

Process of Offering Forgiveness

1. Make four lists. Column one, how the offender hurt you. Column 2: how you felt regarding the hurt. Column 3, list the ramifications. Forth Column, list your sinful reactions to the offence.
2. Admit to God how you felt regarding the offense.
3. Admit to God that you have been holding this person guilty for this act.
4. Admit to God that your reactions to this offense, and the person, are sin.
5. Claim God's forgiveness for your reactions (sin).
6. Extend forgiveness, in prayer before God, for the hurt this person has caused you.
7. Put the offender in God's hands and join Him in doing what He wants to bring healing.
8. By choice, your feelings most likely will not match, live each day as a freeman.
9. Agree with God that you are willing to be reconciled to the offender and allow Him to love the offender through you.

You are now free, go now and seek forgiveness for your part! (See Seeking Forgiveness chapter)

How to Seek Forgiveness

Purpose Statement

Humility breeds freedom. When someone chooses to seek the forgiveness of another they have hurt, they provide an opportunity to demonstrate the power of Christ's forgiveness. It is a great way to reveal the gospel. Seeking forgiveness is simply this; honestly reviewing how you hurt another by words, actions, or lack of action. It is going to that person (preferably in person) and saying, "I was wrong" for whatever you did to create pain in their lives – then asking for their forgiveness. Forgiveness is "giving freedom before the offended has the opportunity to unveil bitterness."

Seeking Forgiveness Is Not . . .

It is not going to another to "put things behind you" or "get the monkey off your back." It is not "smoothing over" what you did, and it is certainly not bringing up their actions that "caused" you to hurt them. It is humbling yourself before them, confessing your sin and not considering their sin, or hurt, done unto you.

Process of Seeking Forgiveness

1. Make three lists. Column one, who you hurt. Column 2: how you hurt them. Column 3, how you acted toward them after you hurt them.
2. Make sure you "extend forgiveness" before God if they hurt you.
3. Pray through the "Seeking Forgiveness" list.

4. Rehearse what and how you are going to say it.
5. Reject any defense, excuses, or blame.
6. Pray and get counsel for the "right timing."
7. Call the person to set a time. The phone conversation should go something like this; Mom, I am calling to find a time to get with you regarding seeking your forgiveness for some things I believe I have done to hurt you. What is the best time for you?
8. If they want to do it on the phone, delay. Plead to do this in person. If they refuse to meet with you in person or circumstances dictate that you can't, ask for a phone time that is best for them.
9. When the meeting starts, thank them for allowing you to do this.
10. Go down column two and three and say "I was wrong for _____, would you forgive me for this?" Wait for the answer and repeat this process until you have completed the list.
11. At the end of the meeting, thank them again. Now ask them is there anything you can do to assist in restoring the relationship. If the request is reasonable, do what they ask of you.

You have now completed the forgiveness cycle. Be blessed!

Acts of Rebellion

❧✝☙

"Woe to them! For they have gone the way of Cain, and for pay they have rushed headlong into the error of Balaam, and perished in the rebellion of Korah. These are the men who are hidden reefs in your love feasts when they feast with you without fear, caring for themselves; clouds without water, carried along by winds; autumn trees without fruit, doubly dead, uprooted; wild waves of the sea, casting up their own shame like foam; wandering stars, for whom the black darkness has been reserved forever."
(Jude 1:11-13)

ENCOURAGEMENT: Their trees are without fruit - The idea here is substantially the same as that expressed by Peter (2 Peter 2:17, KJV) when he talks about false teachers as being "wells without water." Jude also wrote about false teachers being "clouds without water, carried along by winds." So, there would be no shedding down of refreshing rain upon the earth. Such wells and clouds only disappoint expectations. A fruit-promising tree, whose fruit always dries up, would be useless. Therefore, rebels head to the local dry silk flower shop to buy plastic fruit and glue it to their tree. The words "no fruit" occur nowhere else in the New Testament. Properly, it means, "autumn" and the expression here denotes "trees of autumn." In other words, these are trees stripped of leaves and green in color, trees on which there is no fruit. The idea here is not that the tree never bore fruit; the Greek text reveals a tree in a constant state of "autumn" – stripped of growth. Rebellious people are naked trees of autumn as contrasted with the bloom of spring and the dense foliage of summer. Their acts of rebellion stop the flow of "sap" within the tree to bear forth the fruit of righteousness. This prayer stands against the constant state of "autumn" in a person's life.

PRAYER

My precious Heavenly Father, I understand that Your Holy Scriptures state that rebellion is as the sin of witchcraft. I confess that my rebellious sin of _____ is an act of witchcraft before Your Holy throne. I ask for You to reclaim all the ground I've given to the enemy and his kingdom by this act of rebellion. I open my heart and mind to the purifying redemption of the blood of You, Jesus. I ask that You would fill the very place that this sin occupied with Your power, presence, and perfection. I pray that the Holy Spirit would fill me with the fruit of the Spirit and cause a manifestation of that fruit to come forth in my life. May the Holy Spirit grant me the power to submit my mind, will, and emotions over to You. I pray for strength from Heaven to fill my mind with the ability to resist the temptations and attacks the enemy will throw my way. I believe Your power will chase the enemy away as I am praying this prayer. It is in the mighty name of Christ I pray. **Amen.**

Renouncing Pride

✿†✿

*"For all that is in the world, the lust of the flesh and
the lust of the eyes and the boastful pride of life, is not from the Father,
but is from the world."*
(1 John 2:16)

ENCOURAGEMENT: The pride of life - the word properly used here means: *vulgar or boasting*, and then, *arrogance or pride*. It refers to whatever tends to promote pride or a list of things that demonstrate pride (such as - the boastful way of dress, acting as if wealthy, speaking as if better than others, or simply thinking oneself to be able to cope without God). It is not from the Father. In Greek, it means *to offend God*. It is not the nature of true Christians to seek these things, nor can a proud heart even open itself to the things of God. The sincere Christian has humility as their armor or covering. This is evidence of friendship with the world (James 4:4). People of pride are setting themselves up to have a hostile relationship with God. Pride is listed fourth of the seven things "God hates" (Prov. 6:16-19). This prayer assists the believer to stand against such deceptive ways of the enemy.

PRAYER

I pray, this day, in the blessed name and power of the Holy Spirit. It is in the humility of Jesus that I claim victory over my sin of pride. I now renounce and confess the sin of my prideful act of_____. I ask You, Lord Jesus, to reclaim the ground my pride has yielded over to Satan and his kingdom. May the precious blood of Jesus wash me clean from the ramifications of my sinful pride. I ask You, Lord, to grant to me the grace and peace of a yielded, humble heart before You. Here and now, I *resist all prideful demonic attempts that the enemy may use to rule over me. In the name of my Lord Jesus Christ, I ask that You, Father, would put a new heart of humility in me. I give You Your right and prerogative to manifest in me the gentleness of Your Spirit. Take all harshness away that this pride has formed in me. May I entrust my thoughts to You with a new heart and may the Holy Spirit captivate all of my thoughts and actions. I choose, this day, to walk in the integrity of Jesus. It is only in His name that I pray this.* **Amen.**

Renouncing Sexual Bonds

"Food is for the stomach, and the stomach is for food, but God will do away with both of them. Yet the body is not for immorality, but for the Lord, and the Lord is for the body. Now God has not only raised the Lord, but will also raise us up through His power."
(1 Corinthians 6:13-14,).

ENCOURAGEMENT: *Yet the body is not* – the meaning from the Greek: *"the body is not designed for perusing sexual desires for selfish reasons, but to be devoted to the Lord."* The remainder of this section is occupied with an argument against indulgence in sex, a crime in which the Corinthians were particularly guilty. Paul is simply guarding the Corinthians against temptation and settling the morality of the question on this immovable foundation and doctrine of God. The first argument, stated here, is that the body of humanity was designed by its Maker to be devoted to Him and should be consecrated (set apart) for a pure and holy life. Therefore, we are bound to devote our bodies, as well as our rational powers, to the service of the Lord alone. This passage also states that we have no power in and of ourselves to contain this passion; it must be yielded to the power of Christ in us. This prayer renounces sinful sexual unions we have had with others outside of God's holy institution of marriage.

PRAYER

I confess and renounce my sinful sexual union with _____ as a sin against You, my body, and _____ (the person you had the bond with). I ask that the cleansing blood of Jesus free me from the guilt and ground I've given by my sexual union with _____. I renounce all bonding with *this person that took place in the sexual act and I ask You to free me from the consequences of that bonding. I renounce all wicked and demonic holds that have a claim against me because of that sexual sin. In the name of Jesus, I break and renounce all transfer of evil that could have taken place.*

If you lead me to reconcile with this person, I pray for the willingness and strength to do so. I pray that You would give me the words and the proper attitude to seek their forgiveness. I pray that You would use this unholy bond we had as a venue to lead _____ to repentance and freedom as You did with me. I pray for complete freedom and forgiveness on their behalf. I cover both of us in the protective blood of Jesus Christ. It is in the power of Your Holy name that I pray. **Amen.**

Sinful Habits

ഏ✝ഏ

"We are destroying speculations and every lofty thing raised up against the knowledge of God, and we are taking every thought captive to the obedience of Christ, and we are ready to punish all disobedience, whenever your obedience is complete."
(2 Corinthians 10:5).

ENCOURAGEMENT: *Destroying speculations* - the word used here is probably in the sense of a *device, stronghold, or habit*. It refers to all the plans of a wicked world, the various systems of false philosophy, and the personal sins that rise against God. The various systems of false philosophy were so embedded (in the Corinthians, in this case) that they might be called the stronghold of the enemies of God. The reality of sinful habits is that of resisting the Gospel. These "bad habits" simply get in the way of the flow of the Holy Spirit working in and through us as Christians. All are obedient 100% of the time. The question is, "To what?" Habits are gods that rise against the face of God, the Father. They are not just "bad habits" to God; they are covenant agreements (strongholds) with idols. This prayer breaks those bonds with those idols.

PRAYER

I come before You with the joy of my Salvation. It is only in the power and name of Jesus Christ that I pray. Father, I ask that you would deliver me from my habitual sin of _____. I state and choose to believe that this habit is sinful toward You and my body. I understand that this habit has given the enemy ground or place for the rule of darkness to continue to hold me from serving You with a clear conscience. I pray that You would wash me clean from the soil and power of this habitual sin. I do ask that You would reclaim all the ground that I've given over to the enemy because of this sin. In the blessed name of Jesus, I ask that You would remove any foothold the enemy has placed in my life as a result of this continued sin. If the enemy has placed darkness around me due to this sin, I ask that You would chase it away with Your everlasting power and presence. I claim back this ground for the use and purpose of Your kingdom. I lay my life (body, soul, and spirit) at Your altar for service in Jesus' name. I thank You for the freedom You have given me this day. It is through Your act of forgiveness and redemption of the Cross that I pray – Amen.

Sin of Forefathers

❦✝❧

"If you address as Father the One who impartially judges according to each one's work, conduct yourselves in fear during the time of your stay on earth; knowing that you were not redeemed with perishable things like silver or gold from your futile way of life inherited from your forefathers, but with precious blood, as of a lamb unblemished and spotless, the blood of Christ."
(1 Peter 1:17-19)

ENCOURAGEMENT: Here, the word redeemed means: *they were rescued from their sins, the sins of their forefathers, and death by the blood of Christ* (or the life of Christ offered as a sacrifice). It was that which God was pleased to accept in the place of the sinner's punishment, both present, and forefather, as answering the same great ends in His eternal purpose. The principles of this Truth and justice could certainly be stated that without Christ's redemptive act, the guilt and punishment passed down as an inheritance from our forefathers would send us to the place of torment. If the redemptive act of Christ is so, then there is no obstacle to our Salvation or personal freedom; and we might, on repentance, be consistently pardoned and taken to heaven or given personal freedom here on earth.

PRAYER

Through Jesus and His proclaimed redemptive blood, I affirm that I have been redeemed from all consequences of the empty way of life handed down to my family and me through the sins and failures of my forefathers on my father's side of the family. I specifically renounce strongholds of _____ (particular sins you struggle with). In the blessed name of Jesus,

I forbid any powers of darkness from controlling me or the family members for whom I am responsible because of ground given by my father's generational lineage, which extends back three and even four generations. I renounce such claim the enemy might have because of their footholds. I stand firm on the death, burial, and resurrection of Jesus Christ as a fully sufficient release from their actions of rebellion that came against You Father. I know, by Your Word, that the enemy works through generational oppression. Because of this insight, I stand against the generational pattern of deception he uses to bind me and my future generations. Jesus, I now join You in Your stated truth that all the works of the enemy have been stopped as a result of this prayer. I pray by faith that the work of the Cross and co-crucifixion are at work to bring me and my family daily deliverance from these generational sins. It is through and for the name of Jesus that I pray these things. Amen.

Prayer for Illness

"Also the people from the cities in the vicinity of Jerusalem were coming together, bringing people who were sick or afflicted with unclean spirits, and they were all being healed."
(Acts 5:16)

ENCOURAGEMENT: Sickness is one of the main tools of the enemy. Why? Because the human body is depraved and belongs to the dirt. Our spirit and soul are what goes on to be with the Lord when we die; our physical bodies are to lie in the grave for decay and destruction – because they belong to the ways of wickedness. Therefore, this is why our bodies are the most outward tool or vessel available to the enemy. We must come against these attacks of the enemy in this arena. Jesus did not change His approach and ability to heal the sick. Today, stand on the promise and truth that God can heal the human body – if He chooses to do so. If you pray and God chooses to leave the illness in place, accept it as divine grace and purpose.

PRAYER

I now ask in the name of my Husband, Jesus Christ, through the power offered in the Holy Spirit, to stand strong in the allotted weaknesses I suffer. If this is an attack by the enemy, give me the same courage You gave Paul – that I would embrace that Your power is perfected in my weaknesses. If this illness results from poor choices I am making, I ask the Holy Spirit to make a thorough search in and around me. I acknowledge that I am not my body. I aline myself with the Truth that my identity is in Jesus Christ. May the Holy Spirit sanctify my mind & body according to your Holy will. I pray that the enemy is kept from using this illness as works of darkness. I invite the Lord Jesus Christ, by the power of the Holy Spirit, to use this weakness to accomplish Your mission. If it is Your will to heal me of this illness, I accept the redeeming healing power within my mortal body. If you choose to leave this weakness in place, by the power of Christ, I accept Your will concerning this - unto death if You so choose. I do ask that you draw me unto Yourself amid this physical trial for my spiritual growth.

Thank You for loving me despite this weakness. Your grace is sufficient for me. I will rejoice in and through this trial. On the days this trial is difficult to bear, cause me to see that Your grace is enough in this time of weakness. Please grant me the wisdom and grace of protection from the lies and deception the enemy throws at me when I suffer. I ask that You use this situation to teach me how to stand – willingly – in the power and grace You offer, as one of Your children. Release in me the power of Christ to make use of this infirmity to minister to others. I worship You and give You thanks in the name of our Lord Jesus Christ. I commit to stand bold amid all my weaknesses. **Amen**

Sensing an Evil Spirit

✤

"And the man, in whom was the evil spirit, leaped on them and subdued all of them and overpowered them, so that they fled out of that house naked and wounded."
(Acts 19:6)

ENCOURAGEMENT: First things first - Christians cannot be possessed by an evil spirit. We can, on the other hand, be oppressed. Many "doctrinal" theologians believe Christians can be possessed. Don't buy into such cheap doctrines. You, or your loved ones, were bought with a price – that is, if you/they have had a born-again experience. No man can serve two masters. A life divided against itself will fall. When Christ came into your mortal body, He did a first-rate cleaning job. Oppression is much different than possession. Possession requires ownership, while oppression requires a vessel willing to choose sin. Big difference! It is why we pray against oppressive spirits that rise against the true and holy knowledge of God.

PRAYER

In Your name Lord, Jesus Christ, and by the power of Your blood, I come against any wicked spirit that may be harassing me with lies. I ask Lord that You would cause these wicked spirits to flee, along with their manipulative lies & oppressive ways. Lord Jesus, I ask that You replace any thoughts that the enemy has occupied with Your thoughts. I accept Your love, acceptance, and forgiveness. I ask the Holy Spirit to search out all control points I have yielded to the enemy's lies.

As in Paul's case, if Your sovereignty uses these 'messengers of Satan' to buffet me, give me the wisdom & power to allow Your work to be completed in me. If there are willful or covert sins you are addressing within my life, empower me to accept this revelation quickly, submit to You, and move on with releasing Your Life within me.

If these harassments are not a part of Your Divine purpose, please evict these dark powers from my presence. I stand boldly in and through You. I ask for a release of being focused on darkness and fear. I refuse to give any credit to the enemy or his dark forces. I acknowledge and accept that You are the creator of all things, that Your power is perfected in weaknesses, You alone can chase darkness back to dark places, and no human or spirit can rise above Your position as God. Father, I believe You are God. Jesus, I believe You are God. And…Holy Spirit, I believe You are God. I believe the Word of God is Holy and is absolute Truth. I believe that Satan is Your greatest enemy, and he has no power over Your Trinity. As with the case of Your servant Job, empower me NEVER to curse You in any way. May my resolve be like his.

I stand with You in victory. I stand in Your Sovereign's will. I will set my focus on things above – not on this earth.   Amen

Affirming Salvation

✞

"That if you confess with your mouth Jesus as Lord, and believe in your heart that God raised Him from the dead, you will be saved; for with the heart a person believes, resulting in righteousness, and with the mouth he confesses, resulting in salvation."
(Romans 10:9-10)

ENCOURAGEMENT: This Scripture (from the Greek text) properly means to "speak what agrees with something which others speak or maintain." It is to confess, profess, or express our agreement or "covenant contract" with what God declares as Truth and what He declares to be the way, the Truth, and the Life. It denotes a public declaration, or consent, expressed here by the words, "with the mouth." So then, a profession of authentic indwelling Christianity denotes a public declaration of our agreement with what God has declared. Specifically, it extends to all His declarations about our lost state, our sin, and our need for a Savior. It also means agreeing with God's doctrines about His Nature, Holiness, and Law; the Savior and the Holy Spirit; the necessity of a change of heart and holiness of life; the grave and the judgment; and heaven and hell. It respects the Redeemer doctrine, which is the main and leading doctrine put here by way of God's high and raised position. The fact is all those who have accepted Christ as their Lord and Savior (those who truly believe from their heart) will publicly express their consent to this - it is simply to declare our agreement with God on all spoken Truth. This is the litmus test of true Christians: Are they public about their faith? This prayer assists in this proclamation.

PRAYER

I affirm that my only hope for love, acceptance, the forgiveness of sins, and eternal life rests on the finished work of You, Lord Jesus. I entrust my eternal destiny fully into Your hands and to the ministry of the Holy Spirit who has sealed my Salvation. On the days I question my Salvation, I pray that You would affirm and confirm the day You sent the Holy Spirit to live within me. In the power of Your shed blood, I here and now renounce and disown all the ways the enemy comes to steal the joy of my Salvation. If for any reason You are convicting me that the Holy Spirit does not indwell me, I ask You to lead me into receiving Your Life today. I confess that You Jesus are God. I agree with the doctrines of being born into sin. I believe all non-indwelt individuals must receive the Holy Spirit into their mortal bodies by confessing their sinful state. I renounce that following You is authentic Salvation while believing that an authentic born-again experience is needed. Therefore, if I am not authentically born-again, I receive Your Life and redemption today. However, if I am saved, I reaffirm my Salvation in You with these affirmations.

Thank you for hearing my prayer today. I am blessed to call you my Father. Jesus, I am joyful to call You my Husband. Holy Spirit, I am overwhelmed with hope for providing indwelling Life. I confess with my mouth that Jesus is Lord, that You Father raised Him from the dead, that You have saved me, and I am now filled with Your Righteousness. It is in the blessed name of our Savior, I pray. **Amen.**

Relational Walls

➋†➌

"Therefore I, the prisoner of the Lord, implore you to walk in a manner worthy of the calling with which you have been called, with all humility and gentleness, with patience, showing tolerance for one another in love, being diligent to preserve the unity of the Spirit in the bond of peace. There is one body and one Spirit, just as also you were called in one hope of your calling; one Lord, one faith, one baptism, one God and Father of all who is over all and through all and in all."
(Ephesians 4:1-6)

ENCOURAGEMENT: The unity of the Spirit - a united spirit or oneness of spirit. This refers to more than the fact there is one Holy Spirit; it also refers to the unity of affection, confidence, and love that is to exist between all Bridal members of Christ (Christians). It means authentic Christians should be united in mind and affection and not be split into groups and doctrinal factions. It may be implied here, as is undoubtedly true, that such a unity would only be possible by and through the Holy Spirit; and that, as there is but one Spirit who unites our hearts back to God, we certainly ought to have the same goal for each other. There is always the danger of division where people are brought together in a particular society. There are so many different views of God by way of intellect and feeling, the model of education and training, and personal interpretation, all of which contribute to the constant danger of division. Satan has used these tools of the tree of knowledge for many generations to bring about relational walls that separate the Body of Christ. Pray against them!

PRAYER

Dear Lord Jesus, I believe and know that relationships are for the divine purpose of revealing Your message of Truth to those You bring into our lives. I boldly stand before Your throne. I appropriate Your power and authority. You have given me the honor to be a Child of God. I am a lover of Your Truth and Righteousness, and it is because of that, I believe love can pull down the walls, relationships, and barriers that Satan and his kingdom are building between Your children. I pray that You would demolish all the destructive strongholds the kingdom of darkness has been able to erect between Body members of Christ. I ask for You to unleash the mighty power of the loving heavenly Father on any relationship I have allowed to go unreconciled. Release in me the ability to make all relationships about You, not me/us. I ask that the Holy Spirit manifest Your fruit of love, joy, peace, patience, kindness, goodness, faithfulness, gentleness, and self-control in each of the relationships You have given me. By the measurement of faith, You have given to me, I pray for the healing power of the true and living Word to break down all strongholds in our relationships that rise against Your hand. I ask for healing in any disruptive relationship I have. If You lead me to seek their forgiveness for anything I have done to hurt them, cause me to be willing. Please release healing words as I seek their forgiveness. I ask all this in Your mighty name. **Amen.**

Death of A Loved One

✣

"Another of the disciples said to Him, 'Lord, permit me first to go and bury my father.' But Jesus said to him, 'Follow Me, and allow the dead to bury their dead."
(Matthew 8:21-22)

ENCOURAGEMENT: *Let the dead bury their dead* – in this passage, the word "dead" is used in two different senses. It is an absurdity but is used to convey the idea very distinctly. Often, the Jews used the word "dead" to express indifference toward a "thing" - or rather, to show that "the thing" does not influence them. Consequently, *to be dead to the world; to be dead to the law,* Rom. 7:4; and to be *dead to sin,* Rom. 6:11, means that the world, law, and sin have no influence or control over us; that we are free from them, and act *"as though they were not."* A body in the grave is unaffected by the showiness and vanity; by the cheerfulness and partying; and by the ambition and splendor that may be near the gravesite. They see not its beauty, hear not the voices of family and friends, and are not won by the memorials offered to them. This is the group to whom the Savior refers here. Christ is in effect saying: Let the uninterested people in My work and who are *"dead in sin"* take care of those already dead. Meaning, once dead, the individuals and or spiritual forces that are dead to the power of Christ deal with their own. Plus, once they have passed from this life to the next, they join the dead on the other side. Secondly, the living humans have no power or prerogative to change their eternal condition once they enter the other side. He leaves the viewers with, *Now, follow Me.*

While many religious groups adhere to the demonic doctrines that humans contain the ability to talk to the dead, place blessings upon them, or move them to higher levels of spirituality, they do not. As soon as a person passes from human life to the spiritual realm, the door is closed on all communications. Some might talk to their dead, but they cannot hear a word being said. The devil uses this modality to get humans to talk to him. It's called sorcery. Meaning, since the dead bury their dead, they are bordering on witchcraft when humans talk to their dead loved ones. While compassion understands their "need" to talk to loved ones who have passed, Jesus made it evident that all authentic believers should only talk to God the Father, God the Son, and God the Holy Spirit. Any other attempt to communicate with angels or the dead is ringing the phone line to the demonic realm.

PRAYER

Dear Lord Jesus, I now acknowledge the power and presence of Your life in and around me. I stand firm in the fact and truth that _____ is alive and well in the hands of our Father. If _____ was not a true indwelt believer, grant me the grace to process this potential reality. Please do not allow me to pretend they were saved for my comfort. I agree and align myself with what You said, "allow the dead to bury their dead." I accept this truth to mean that I should not allow the enemy to use death to distract me from living in and through You. By the power of Your spoken Word, please bring closure to my grieving process. By faith, I accept _____'s death and know that You will be using their passing as a tool of sharing the Gospel with those who need to know You. I choose not to focus on questions surrounding their death or the death itself. I take this time to reaffirm my commitment to serving You and You alone. I will go on with the life You have given me. I stand against the ways of the enemy in tempting me to focus on death instead of life. I claim now all the Truth and Victory You offer through this difficult time. I pray only in the blessed name of Jesus Christ and His redemptive and healing ways. Amen

ARMOR OF GOD

Belt of Truth

❧✝☙

*"Stand firm therefore, HAVING GIRDED YOUR
LOINS WITH TRUTH."*
(Ephesians 6:14)

PRAYER

In the name of the Lord Jesus Christ, I claim the protection of the belt of Truth, having buckled it securely around my waist. I pray the protection of the belt of Truth over my personal life, my home and family, and the ministry God has appointed for my life. I use the belt of Truth directly against Satan and his kingdom of darkness. I aggressively embrace Him, who is the Truth, the Lord Jesus Christ, as my strength and protection from all of Satan's deceptions. I desire that the Truth of Your Word shall constantly gain a deeper place in my life. I pray that the Truth of Your Word maybe my heart's delight to study and memorize.

I accept your forgiveness for the sin of not speaking the truth. Show me any way in which I am being deceived. By the Holy Spirit of Truth, open the Scriptures to my understanding and guide me into the practical understanding of Your Words of Truth. I ask the Holy Spirit to warn me before I deceive anyone. I also ask the Holy Spirit to protect me from believing Satan's lies. Thank You, Lord, for making my local church a pillar and foundation for Your Truth in my life. Cause me to relate to my church and give protection and help to others.

Lord Jesus, I see You as the Way, the Truth, and the Life in me who can stand against the lies and fiery missiles of the devil. Thank You for providing this part of the armor for me. I understand it is protected through Your power. **Amen.**

Righteousness

ଚ∻†∻ଚ

"HAVING GIRDED YOUR LOINS WITH TRUTH, and HAVING
PUT ON THE BREASTPLATE OF RIGHTEOUSNESS."
(Ephesians 6:14b)

"Yes, truth is lacking; and he who turns aside from evil makes himself a prey. Now the LORD saw, and it was displeasing in His sight that there was no justice. And He saw that there was no man, and was astonished that there was no one to intercede; then His own arm brought salvation to Him, And His righteousness upheld Him. He put on righteousness like a breastplate, and a helmet of salvation on His head; And He put on garments of vengeance for clothing And wrapped Himself with zeal as a mantle."
(Isaiah 59:15-17)

PRAYER

In the name of the Lord Jesus Christ, I put on the breastplate of righteousness. At this moment, I reject any dependence I may have upon my goodness or self-righteousness. I embrace the righteousness that is mine by faith in the Lord Jesus Christ. I look to the Holy Spirit to be effecting righteous actions, pure thoughts, and holy attitudes in my life. I hold up the righteous life of the Lord Jesus Christ to defeat Satan and his kingdom. I affirm that my victory is won and lived out by my Savior, who lives within me. I eagerly ask and expect that the Lord Jesus Christ shall live His righteousness through me. Through the precious blood of Christ, cleanse me of all my sins of omission and commission. Let me walk in the holy and clean manner that honors You, God, which defeats the world, the flesh, and the devil, through the power of the blood of Jesus Christ, my Lord. Amen.

Peace

ஒ†ஜ

"And with your feet fitted with the gospel of peace as a firm footing."
(Ephesians 6:15)

"Peace I leave with you; My peace I give to you; not as the world gives do I give to you. Do not let your heart be troubled, nor let it be fearful."
(John 14:27)

"But now in Christ Jesus you who formerly were far off have been brought near by the blood of Christ. For He Himself is our peace…"
(Ephesians 2:13-14a).

PRAYER

Loving heavenly Father, by faith and in the name of the Lord Jesus Christ, I put on the shoes of peace. I accept Your declaration that I am justified and have peace with You. May my mind grasp that wondrous Truth with ever-increasing awareness. Thank You, Lord, that I need not carry any anxiety or suffer from inner torment or turmoil. Thank You, Lord Jesus Christ, that You have invited me to make all of my needs known to You through prayer. Teach me to wait in Your presence until Your inner peace comes as a practical experience, which transcends my human understanding and destroys all anxiety. I desire to know the strong presence of Your peace. May You walk and live through me in those moments when I am tempted to find false peace in the world.

With all my heart, I choose to be obedient to Your will by living the life of Christ in me. I take the shoes of peace in the name of the Lord Jesus Christ. By faith, I choose to put them on and walk in them this day forward. Enable me to walk in Truth and the fullness of Your peace. **Amen.**

Faith

"In addition to all, taking up the shield of faith with which you will be able to extinguish all the flaming arrows of the evil one."
(Ephesians 6:16)

PRAYER

Loving heavenly Father, I take by faith the protection of the shield of faith – Your presence. I count upon Your holy presence to surround me like a capsule, offering total protection from all of Satan's flaming arrows. Grant me power and strength to walk in Your presence. Empower me to accept Your refining purpose in allowing any of Satan's arrows to pass through and even to praise You for it. Supernaturally, cause me to concentrate upon Your presence in my life and not the enemy's tricks of deception.

In the name of my Lord Jesus Christ, I claim the protection of the holy angels, the Holy Spirit, and Christ Himself from the assaults of Satan's kingdom. May Your ministering angels be present to interfere with the strategy of Satan to harm my family, my fellow Christian body members, and me. I appropriate the victory of the blood of the Lord Jesus Christ and hold it against the advances of the evil one. With gratitude and praise, in the name of the Lord Jesus Christ, I rejoice in Your victory. Amen.

Sword

⊱✝⊰

"Take . . .the sword of the Spirit, which is the Word of God"
(Ephesians 6:17b)

PRAYER

In the blessed name of the Lord Jesus Christ, I lay hold of the Sword of the Spirit, the living Word of God. I embrace its inerrant message of Truth and power. I humbly ask the Holy Spirit to guide me into a true understanding of the message of the Word. Grant to me the discipline and dedication to study the Word, to saturate my mind with its Truth and power, and to speak it out boldly when You call upon me to do so.

In the name of Jesus Christ and by the ministry of the Holy Spirit, grant to me the wisdom to always apply the Word against the enemy. May I use the Word to defeat Satan and to advance the cause of Christ into the very realm Satan attempts to make claims.

Father, by the power of the Holy Spirit, open my mind to Your Scriptures that I might understand Your Word. I pray that as I read it, You will guide me into the practical elements of what You are saying. I understand that without You revealing the true meaning of the Word, I will not understand it in my strength. I choose to deny myself and pick up my Cross and follow the leading of Your Word. In Jesus' name, I pray. Amen.

Salvation

✥

"The LORD is my rock and my fortress and my deliverer, My God, my rock, in whom I take refuge; my shield and the horn of my Salvation, my stronghold."
(Psalm 18:2)

PRAYER

Loving heavenly Father, I take by faith the helmet of Salvation. I recognize that my Salvation is in the Person of Your Son, the Lord Jesus Christ. I cover my mind with His; I desire that He put His mind within me. Let my thoughts be His thoughts. I open my mind completely and only to the control of the Lord Jesus Christ. I replace my own selfish and sinful thoughts with His. I reject every projected thought of Satan and his demons, and instead, I request the mind of the Lord Jesus Christ. Grant me the wisdom to discern thoughts from the world, my fleshly self, and Satan's kingdom.

I believe: Jesus is Your Son, He died on the Cross for my sins, and Jesus is God. I believe in: the Trinity; You, as the Father; Jesus, as the Son; and the Holy Spirit. I confess that I have been a sinner – totally separated from You. I choose to accept Your forgiveness for my sins through the power of the blood of Jesus that was shed for me on the Cross. I now ask that you send the Holy Spirit to live inside my mortal body. (Pause for a moment)

I praise You, heavenly Father, that I may know the mind of Christ as I hide Your Word within my heart and mind. Open my heart to love Your Word. Grant to me the ability and capacity to memorize large portions of it. May Your Word be ever over my mind like a helmet of strength, which Satan's projected thoughts cannot penetrate. Cause me to allow the Holy Spirit (the Life of Christ) within me to fulfill the discipline of daily living to appropriate Your Salvation. These things I lay before You in the precious name of my new Savior, the Lord Jesus Christ. **Amen!**

Full Armor

✣

"Put on the whole armor of God that you may be able to stand against the wiles of the devil."
(Ephesians 6:11, NKJV)

PRAYER

Heavenly Father, I desire to be obedient by being strong in the Lord and the power of Your might. I see this is Your will and purpose for me. I recognize it is essential to put on the armor that You have provided. I do so now with gratitude and praise that You have provided all I need to stand in the victory against Satan and his kingdom. Grant me wisdom to discern the tactics and sneakiness of Satan's strategy against me. Enable me to wrestle in the victory against the princes, powers, rulers, and wicked spirits who carry the battle of darkness against me.

I delight in taking the armor. You have provided. By faith, I put it on as effective spiritual protection against the spiritual forces of darkness.

I confidently take the loin girdle of Truth You offer me. I take Him who is the Truth as my strength and protection. I reject Satan's lies and deceiving ways that try to gain an advantage against me. Grant me discernment and wisdom to recognize the subtle deceiving ways Satan seeks to cause me to accept his lies as truth. I desire to believe only in the Truth, live the Truth, speak the Truth, and know the Truth. I worship and praise You, that You lead me only in the ways of Truth. Thank You that Satan cannot stand against the bold use of the Truth.

I embrace the breastplate of righteousness, which you offer me. I eagerly accept it and put it on as my protection. I ask You to cleanse me of all the times I have counted my goodness as being acceptable before You. I bring the righteousness of my Lord directly against all of Satan's works against me.

I embrace the sandals of peace. You have provided. I desire that my feet should stand on the solid rock of peace. You have provided. I claim the peace of God, which is mine through justification. Thank You for not giving me a spirit of fear - but a spirit of love, power, and a sound mind. Thank You that Satan cannot stand against Your peace.

I now lift my shield of faith against all the blazing missiles Satan and his hosts' fire at me. I recognize You are my shield, and in Your incarnation and crucifixion, You took the arrows of the enemy for me. By faith, I count upon You to shield me from above and beneath; my right and my left; and my front and back; that I might be protected, walled in, and encapsulated by you, so that Satan may not be able to hurt or destroy me from fulfilling Your will today. Thank You, Lord Jesus, that You are a complete and perfect shield and that Satan cannot touch me apart from Your sovereign purpose.

I take my helmet of Salvation and choose to put it on. I cover my mind and my thoughts with Your Salvation. I recognize that the Lord Jesus Christ is my Salvation. I invite Your mind to be in me. Let me think Your thoughts; feel Your love and compassion; and discern Your will and leading in all things. May the Salvation of my Lord Jesus meet and defeat all satanic thoughts that come to my mind.

With joy, I take and embrace the Sword of the Spirit, which is the Word of God. I affirm that Your Word is the trustworthy, infallible Word of God. I choose to believe it and to live in its Truth and power. I accept your cleansing from the sin of neglecting Your Word. Empower me to have proficient recall and skill in using Your Word against all of Satan's attacks against me, even as my Lord Jesus used the Word against Satan. I take back any ground the enemy has gained while I was lazy and *disobedient in proclaiming Your Word. Thank You that Satan must retreat from Your Word applied against him.*

Thank You, Father, for prayer. Cause me to keep this armor well-oiled with the power of prayer. I desire to pray at all times with depth and intensity as the Holy Spirit leads me. I reject all fleshly praying as sin. I trust the Holy Spirit to enable me and to intercede for me and through me. All of these petitions, intercessions, and words of praise I offer up before the true and living God in the name and worthy merit of my Lord Jesus Christ. **Amen**

Aggressive Warfare

✾†✿

"For though we walk in the flesh, we do not war according to the flesh, for the weapons of our warfare are not of the flesh, but divinely powerful for the destruction of fortresses. We are destroying speculations and every lofty thing rose up against the knowledge of God, and we are taking every thought captive to the obedience of Christ."
(2 Corinthians 10:3-5)

PRAYER

As a child of You, God, purchased by the blood of the Lord Jesus Christ, I here and now renounce and repudiate all the sins I have ever committed. I also renounce and repudiate all the sins of my ancestors. As one who has been delivered from the power of darkness and translated into the kingdom of Your dear Son, I cancel out all demonic working passed on to me from my ancestors. As one who has been crucified with Jesus Christ and raised to walk in the newness of life, I cancel every oppressive action that Satan may have been put upon me. I announce to Satan and all his forces that Christ became a curse for me when He hung on the Cross. As one who has been crucified and raised with Christ and now sits with Him in heavenly places, I renounce any and every way in which Satan may claim ownership of me. I declare myself to be eternally and completely signed over and committed to the Lord Jesus Christ. All this I do in the name and authority of the Lord Jesus Christ. Amen.

Armor on Others

≈†≈

"When a strong man, fully armed, guards his own house, his possessions are undisturbed. But when someone stronger than he attacks him and overpowers him, he takes away from him all his armor on which he had relied and distributes his plunder."
(Luke 11:21-22)

ENCOURAGEMENT: When we are fully armed with our spiritual armor, our homes, possessions, and loved ones are protected and undisturbed. But, when the "strongman" (enemy) attacks and we allow him to overpower us, he takes our armor and sets it aside. Most Christians don't even give the Armor of God a second thought. We tend to look at the armor as something that comes with Salvation. That is true, but we are called by the Father to "put it on." Those of us who have come to embrace this truth need to pray for others to do the same. This prayer does just that. Until our fellow loved ones are putting on their armor, we need to pray it on them.

PRAYER

Before I pray that You put on the armor on _____, I now stand in the full armor You have given me. In the name of Your Son, my Warrior, and Protector, I ask that You surround me with the fullness of Your protection. I join _____ in putting on the full armor of God. We agree together to walk in the belt of Truth, the breastplate of righteousness, the sandals of peace, the shield of faith, the helmet of Salvation, and the Sword of the Spirit. We stand together in being covered in the precious blood of the Lord Jesus Christ and the protection within prayer.

I ask You, Heavenly Father, to assign holy angels to watch over and protect _____. I invite the Holy Spirit to minister to every part of their being. Remind _____ to come to You when troubled. If they are authentically indwelt by You, please remind them of the confirmation of their Salvation. Only You know if _____ is truly a Christian. If not, I pray You would draw _____ unto Yourself. I pray You would fill _____ with Your confidence and strength, becoming overwhelmed with Your joy and peace. Until _____ is spiritually old enough to pray effectively, remind me to pray continually until _____ can stand firm in their faith. I pray that You cause _____ to know Your everlasting love. As You pursue _____, may Your power and Life overpower their worldly thoughts. It is in the Name of Jesus, I pray. **Amen.**

DEEDS OF THE FLESH

Flesh

༺✝༻

*"For though we walk in the flesh, we do not war according to the flesh,
for the weapons of our warfare are not of the flesh,
but divinely powerful for the destruction of fortresses.
We are destroying speculations and every lofty
thing rose up against the knowledge of God,
and we are taking every thought captive to the obedience of Christ."*
(2 Corinthians 10:3-5)

PRAYER

Dear Father, I understand that my flesh (the garbage left behind by the "old nature") provides plenty of opportunities to tempt and war against the "spirit man" within me. The flesh is a deadly enemy, capable of temporarily defeating me and keeping me from pleasing You with a holy lifestyle. One of the strategic reasons my flesh is such a deceptive enemy is that it blends into my personality type. I understand my flesh is intertwined with my mind, will, and emotions. I know that before I was saved, it was the control center for my daily decisions. Now that you have saved me, it attempts to deceive me into thinking it is alive and well. The reality is that it is dead.

I choose to believe that my flesh is nothing but old memories of the "old nature" left in my mind because of the "old man" controlling my mind during the years I was unsaved. Your Word tells me in Romans 6:6, "...knowing this that our old self was crucified with Him so that our body of sin might be done away with so that we would no longer be slaves to sin." I claim that the "old self" was crucified with Your son, Jesus Christ, on the day of my Salvation. You did this for my sins to be dealt with for the last time. The Adamic nature (the old self) worked at programming my mind to sin upon impulse, fully knowing there could come a day when the old nature would have to be put to death. I know that once the Adamic nature was removed by death, Satan now has to rely on the programming or memories the "old self" left behind. From the day of my Salvation to the day of my physical death, You God, through the power of the indwelling Holy Spirit, renew my mind from the garbage the "old nature" left behind.

As stated in Your Word (Galatians 5:19-21), I understand the deeds of the flesh are evident in the world around me: "immorality, impurity, sensuality, idolatry, sorcery, enmities, strife, jealousy, outbursts of anger, disputes, dissensions, factions, envying, drunkenness, carousing, and things like these." I accept You are forewarning me that those who practice such things will not inherit the experiential freedom You offer me each day. I embrace Your full Truth regarding my victory over my flesh. In Jesus' name, I pray. **Amen.**

Adultery

"You have heard that it was said, 'YOU SHALL NOT COMMIT ADULTERY'; but I say to you that everyone who looks at a woman with lust for her has already committed adultery with her in his heart."
(Matthew 5:27-28)

PRAYER

In the name of the Lord Jesus Christ, my dear Abba Father, I desire to walk after the Spirit in my daily living. I recognize that the sin of adultery is a direct assault against Your will for my life. I acknowledge before You that every thought and action of adultery that I, or my ancestors, have ever committed is sin. I accept Your unmerited favor and forgiveness You offer me through the blood of Jesus Christ. Through the indwelling Holy Spirit, I recognize that only Your Son can give me the power to fight off these thoughts and temptations. I desire the Holy Spirit to bring all of the work of the crucifixion and resurrection of Jesus into my mind today. Enable me to respond to Your prompting and voice to guard my eyes and mind against looking at others for the fulfillment of my sexual pleasures. I align my mind with Your doctrines for the true purpose of sexual fulfillment – contained for the ordained institution of marriage. I entrust my victory over this fleshly desire today completely into the hands of the Holy Spirit as I choose to let Him take full control of my mind. It is in the blessed name of Jesus Christ, I pray. Amen.

Key Note: If you have committed physical adultery with the opposite sex or same-sex, you need to seek their forgiveness whenever possible. When you do this, take with you a brother who is strong in their walk with Christ. Do not go alone! (review Forgiveness chapters)!

Fornication

☙✝❧

"That you abstain from things sacrificed to idols and from blood and from things strangled and from fornication; if you keep yourselves free from such things, you will do well."
(Acts 15:29)

ENCOURAGEMENT: God challenges us to flee sexual immorality and cleave to Christ, honoring Him with the physical body. Fornication is a result of the sinful fleshly trash the "old nature" left behind (Galatians 5:19) and unsuitable for God's children (Ephesians 5:3). Christ has the ability and power to provide us with all the intimacy needed to "feel" sexually fulfilled. This prayer will help you appropriate this truth.

PRAYER

In the name of the Lord Jesus Christ, my dear Abba Father, I desire to walk after the Spirit in my daily living. I recognize that the sin of fornication is a direct assault against Your will for my life. I acknowledge before You that every immoral thought and action that I, or my ancestors, have ever committed is sin. I accept Your unmerited favor and forgiveness through the blood of Jesus Christ. I recognize it is only Your Son, through the indwelling Holy Spirit, who can fulfill my "feelings" of sexual fulfillment. I desire the Holy Spirit to bring all of the work of the crucifixion and resurrection of Jesus into my mind today. Enable me to respond to Your prompting and voice to guard my eyes and mind against looking at others for the fulfillment of my sexual pleasures. I align my mind with Your doctrines for the true purpose of sexual fulfillment – contained for the ordained institution of marriage. I entrust my victory over this fleshly desire today completely into the hands of the Holy Spirit as I choose to let Him take full control of my mind and body. It is in the blessed name of Jesus Christ, I pray. **Amen.**

Uncleanness

✼☦✼

"Woe to you, scribes and Pharisees, hypocrites! For you are like whitewashed tombs which on the outside appear beautiful, but inside are full of dead men's bones and all uncleanness."
(Matthew 23:27,).

PRAYER

In the name of the Lord Jesus Christ, my dear Abba Father, I desire to walk after the Spirit in my daily living. I recognize that the sins of impure thoughts, so-called "dirty stories," lustful desires, watching pornography and questionable movies, listening to impure music, and reading filthy magazines is a direct assault against Your will for my life. I acknowledge before You that every unclean thought I have is sin. I accept Your unmerited favor and forgiveness through the blood of Jesus Christ. Through the indwelling Holy Spirit, I recognize that Your Son is the only One who can keep me pure. I desire the Holy Spirit to bring all of the work of the crucifixion and resurrection of Jesus into my mind today. Enable me to respond to Your prompting and voice to guard my mind. Today, I entrust my victory over these fleshly thoughts completely into the hands of the Holy Spirit as I choose to let Him take full control of my mind and body. It is in the blessed name of Jesus Christ, I pray. Amen.

Sensuality

∽✝∾

"For from within, out of the heart of men, proceed the evil thoughts, fornications, thefts, murders, and adulteries, deeds of coveting and wickedness, as well as deceit, sensuality, envy, slander, pride and foolishness. All these evil things proceed from within and defile the man."
(Mark 7:21-23)

ENCOURAGEMENT: God gave us the gift of sexual pleasure for the sole purpose of man and woman complementing each other in marriage as "one flesh." God expects us to maintain self-control in all things, not by our efforts, but through the empowerment of the Holy Spirit who lives within us. We have no power to control the sensual urges that reside in our flesh. Only God can control these thoughts and feelings. We need to call for God's redemptive power to deliver us from Satan's trap of sensual seductions.

PRAYER

In the name of the Lord Jesus Christ, Abba Father, I desire to walk after the Spirit in my daily living. I recognize that the sins of seductive behavior are a direct assault against Your will for my life. I acknowledge before You that every act of seduction I have had, or my ancestors had is sin. I accept Your unmerited favor and forgiveness through the blood of Jesus Christ. Through the indwelling Holy Spirit, I recognize that Your Son is the only One who can cause me to act in such a way that is honorable to You. I desire the Holy Spirit to bring all of the work of the crucifixion and resurrection of Jesus into my mind today. Enable me to respond to Your prompting and voice to guard the way I dress, speak, laugh, smile, and gesture. I ask that you cause me to be modest in all things. Remind me that I am not to draw attention to myself. Today, I entrust my victory over these seductive ways completely into the hands of the Holy Spirit as I choose to let Him take full control of my mind and body. It is in the blessed name of Jesus Christ, I pray. Amen

Idolatry

✿✝✿

"For rebellion is as the sin of divination, and insubordination is as iniquity and idolatry. Because you have rejected the word of the LORD, He has also rejected you from being king."
(1 Samuel 15:23)

ENCOURAGEMENT: God shares His glory with no one. Glory is God's shining majesty accompanying His presence. The basic meaning in Hebrew is *heavyweight*. Weight is the same word that is used to define honor. Such honor is recognition of the place of position. The higher the position, the more weight or honor we give to the being in that position. This is why it is a sin to God to put our job, or anything else, in a higher position than the throne of the living God.

PRAYER

Lord Jesus Christ, I desire to walk after the Spirit and serve you in my daily living. I recognize that the sin of idolatry is a direct assault against Your divine nature. I acknowledge before You that the act of _____ is idolatry and sin. If this sin has been passed down to me through my ancestors, I break its power of influence through the blood of Jesus Christ. I accept Your redemption and forgiveness through the work of the Cross. I recognize that it is only Your Son, through the indwelling Holy Spirit, who has the power to cause me to serve You and You alone. I choose to give You all the honor and glory that You deserve. I ask that the Holy Spirit bring the work of the crucifixion and resurrection of Jesus into the areas of my life that these idols have consumed. Enable me to respond to Your prompting and voice to keep my eyes fixed on Jesus. Remind me that I cannot give divine attention to any person, place, or thing, *including myself. Today, I entrust my victory over these idols completely into the hands of the Holy Spirit as I choose to let Him take full control of me. It is in the blessed name of Jesus Christ, I pray.* Amen.

Stubbornness

❧✝❧

"For rebellion is as the sin of divination {witchcraft}, and insubordination is as iniquity and idolatry. Because you have rejected the word of the LORD, He has also rejected you from being king."
(1 Samuel 15:23)

ENCOURAGEMENT: The Bible has strong counsel against a rebellion that manifests itself in drunkenness and the use of illicit drugs. Peter addresses maintaining an alert mind in the face of difficult circumstances (1 Peter 1:13; 5:8). Satan does not want our minds clear and alert. He will tempt us with anything he can to dull our senses. Pornography is a clear example of rebellion and the sin of sorcery. Getting a buzz is witchcraft! Not submitting to authority is witchcraft! All forms of rebellion are the sin of witchcraft. You and I had better call it what it is. Do not soft-sell this sin. Own it, renounce it, and move on.

PRAYER

As a child of You, God, purchased by the blood of the Lord Jesus Christ, I here and now renounce and repudiate all the sins of witchcraft (rebellion) I have ever committed. I also renounce and repudiate all the sins of witchcraft that my ancestors committed. As one who has been delivered from the power of darkness and translated into the kingdom of Your dear Son, I cancel out all demonic working that has been inflicted upon me by the enemy. As one who has been crucified with Jesus Christ and raised to walk in the newness of life, I cancel every act of oppression that Satan uses to tempt me. I announce to Satan and all his forces that Christ became a curse for me when He hung on the Cross and that the sin of witchcraft has no hold on me. As one who has been crucified and raised with Christ and now sits with Him in heavenly places, I renounce any and every way in which Satan may claim false ownership of me. I declare myself to be eternally and completely signed over and committed to the Lord Jesus Christ. All this I do in the name and authority of the Lord Jesus Christ. **Amen.**

Hatred

☙✝❧

"Better is a dish of vegetables where love is than a fattened ox served with hatred."
(Proverbs 15:17)

ENCOURAGEMENT: Take a few moments and make a list of those who have offended you and how they hurt you. Then after completing this assignment, pray through the prayer and place the name of the person you are choosing to forgive in the blanks. Pray boldly and confidently, disregarding your feelings.

PRAYER

Dear Heavenly Father, I acknowledge my forgiveness You offered on the Cross through Jesus Christ. I believe in the power of forgiveness through the indwelling Holy Spirit. I know I have no power to forgive on my own. I bring the reality of Your forgiveness into my life by choosing to forgive those who have hurt me. I renounce all bitterness, anger, contempt, hatred, and vengeance my flesh has displayed against _____ (name of the offender). I acknowledge these reactions as sin. I choose to forgive _____ (name of the offender) in the name of Jesus Christ. I specifically forgive _____ for _____ (offense). I pray the power of the shed blood of Jesus over _____ and ask that You free _____ from guilt and condemnation he/she may feel for hurting me. As one who has been crucified and raised with Christ and now sits with Him in heavenly places, I renounce any and every way Satan has used this offense to hold me hostage. I declare myself eternally and completely free from the ramifications of my bitterness. All this I do in the name and authority of the Lord Jesus Christ. **Amen.**

Quarreling

≽┼≼

"What is the source of quarrels and conflicts among you? Is not the source your pleasures that wage war in your members? You lust and do not have; so you commit murder. You are envious and cannot obtain; so you fight and quarrel. You do not have because you do not ask. You ask and do not receive, because you ask with wrong motives, so that you may spend it on your pleasures."
(James 4:1-3)

ENCOURAGEMENT: The tongue stirs up jealousy and selfish motives. A man who has selfish motives is involved with demonic doctrines. Look at James 3:14-15: *"But if you have bitter jealousy and selfish ambition in your heart, do not be arrogant and so lie against the truth. This wisdom is not that which comes down from above, but is earthly, natural, and demonic."* When a man quarrels, he thinks he is wise by proving he is right. In reality, he is promoting the doctrines of Satan and creating evil disorder. *"For where jealousy and selfish ambition exist, there is disorder and every evil thing"* (James 3:16).

It would be wise for us to renounce all habits of quarreling in which we are involved. Men, in particular, enjoy being right. Therefore, quarreling hits the "top ten" list of vulnerabilities for Christians. Let us go before God and remove all demonic influences this habit/sin of quarreling has brought upon us, our family, and our friends.

PRAYER

As a child of You, God, purchased by the blood of the Lord Jesus Christ, I here and now renounce and repudiate the sin of quarreling (demonic doctrine). I also renounce and repudiate all the sins of quarreling that have been passed down to me through my ancestors. As one who has been delivered from the power of darkness and translated into the kingdom of Your dear Son, I cancel out all demonic doctrines the enemy has placed within my mind. As one who has been crucified with Jesus Christ and raised to walk in the newness of life, I cancel every act of oppression Satan uses to lure me into fighting and quarreling with others. I announce to Satan and all his forces that Christ, and His wisdom, is what is true and right and that the sin of quarreling no longer has any hold on me. I declare myself to be eternally and completely free from the sin of arguing and commit my mind and conversations to the Lord Jesus Christ. All this I do in the name and authority of the Lord Jesus Christ. Amen.

Jealousy

*"For jealousy enrages a man, and
he will not spare in the day of vengeance."*
(Proverbs 6:34).

ENCOURAGEMENT: Nothing describes an angry man more than one filled with resentment, self-attention, or jealousy. Jealousy is the fuel of vengeance. It is the act of stealing another man's prosperity by either mind or possession. Jealousy is an idol. Ezekiel 8:5 helps us to see this: *"Then He said to me, 'Son of man, raise your eyes now toward the north.' So I raised my eyes toward the north, and behold, to the north of the altar gate was this idol of jealousy at the entrance"* When a man chooses to become jealous, he steps into the sin of contradiction and blasphemy (slandering and speaking evil). Acts 13:45 shows us: *"But when the Jews saw the crowds, they were filled with jealousy and began contradicting the things spoken by Paul, and were blaspheming."*

PRAYER

As a child of You, God, purchased by the blood of the Lord Jesus Christ, I here and now renounce and repudiate the sin of jealousy (acts of vengeance). I also renounce and repudiate all the sins of jealousy passed down to me through my ancestors. As one who has been delivered from the power of darkness and translated into the kingdom of Your dear Son, I cancel out all acts of jealousy and vengeance the enemy has placed upon me. As one who has been crucified with Jesus Christ and raised to walk in the newness of life, I cancel every act of oppression Satan uses to seduce me into wanting to be in first place. I announce to Satan and all his forces that Christ is the only One to be in first place. I embrace the

Truth of the importance of being in last place in all things. I declare myself eternally and completely free from the sin of competition. All this I do in the name and authority of the Lord Jesus Christ. Amen.

Anger

✥✝✥

"But now you also, put them all aside: anger, wrath, malice, slander, and abusive speech from your mouth."
(Colossians 3:8)

"Be anxious for nothing, but in everything by prayer and supplication with thanksgiving let your requests be made known to God"
(Philippians 4:6)

"Finally, brethren, whatever is true, whatever is honorable, whatever is right, whatever is pure, whatever is lovely, whatever is of good repute, if there is any excellence and if anything worthy of praise, dwell on these things."
(Philippians 4:8)

ENCOURAGEMENT: Do this, and your wrath will be forever gone; do it not, and you will live a life of destruction, separation, and despair.

PRAYER

As a child of You, God, purchased by the blood of the Lord Jesus Christ, I here and now renounce and repudiate the sins of anger, wrath, malice, slander, and abusive speech. I also renounce and repudiate the wrath passed down to me through my ancestors. As one who has been delivered from the power of darkness and translated into the kingdom of Light, I cancel out all acts of wrath the enemy has placed upon me. As one who has been crucified with Jesus Christ and raised to walk in the newness of life, I cancel every act of oppression with which Satan has burdened me, my family, or the individuals I have a relationship with. I announce to

Satan and all his forces that Christ and the power of His shed blood, has cleansed me from the root of my bitterness. I embrace the Truth of the importance of being anxious for nothing; praying with a thankful heart; and setting my mind on whatever is true, honorable, right, pure, lovely, whatever is of good repute, things of excellence, and anything worthy of Your praise. I do these things only in the strength and power of Jesus Christ through the indwelling life of the Holy Spirit. I declare myself eternally and completely free from the sin of wrath. All this I do in the name and authority of the Lord Jesus Christ. **Amen.**

Arguing

୭✝ଓ

"Let us behave properly as in the day, not in carousing and drunkenness, not in sexual promiscuity and sensuality, not in strife and jealousy."
(Romans 13:13)

ENCOURAGEMENT: People of strife are insolent, which means they are proud, arrogant, and "never wrong" (Proverbs 13:10). They are so bold as to think that the affairs of others belong to them to decide what is right and wrong. Does this sound like "playing god" or what? The root of this person's sin is idolatry – except they think they are God.

PRAYER

I come before You, God, as Your child claiming the power of the blood of the Lord Jesus Christ. I here and now renounce and repudiate the sin of strife. I also renounce and repudiate the strife that has been passed down to me through my ancestors. As one who has been delivered from the power of darkness and translated into the kingdom of Light, I cancel out all acts of strife the enemy has used in my life. Today, I acknowledge to You that this sin has caused me to be a child who separates, causes divisions, argues, is adversarial, hot-tempered, and even attempts to do Your job in deciding what is right and wrong. I see the ramifications the sin of strife has brought upon my relationships. I am now willing to restore any relationship You call me to reconcile. As one who has been born-again and brought into the unity of the Life of Christ, I cancel every act of oppression that Satan has introduced to my family and me, as well as to the individuals to whom I have used the sin of strife in bringing separation. I announce to Satan and all his forces that Christ and the power of His shed blood, has cleansed me from the sin of acting as God. I embrace the Truth of the importance of being unified with the body of Christ. I do these things only in the strength and power of Jesus Christ through the indwelling life of the Holy Spirit. I declare myself eternally and completely free from the sin of strife. All this I do in the name and authority of the Lord Jesus Christ. **Amen.**

Bad Doctrines

✞

"For there must also be factions {heresies} among you, so that those who are approved may become evident among you."
(1 Corinthians 11:19)

ENCOURAGEMENT: Strife is the action of wrangling words. Heresies are the doctrines that come out of a man who is filled with strife. Christians who teach heresies purpose to divide and split up discussions into two parts. This sin causes church splits, marital separation, rebellious children, broken business partnerships, and divisions in friendships. This sin strikes at the essential unity of the body of Christ and divides that which Jesus Christ works so diligently to bring unity and hope.

PRAYER

I come before You, God, as Your child claiming the power of the blood of the Lord Jesus Christ. Here and now, I renounce and repudiate the sin of heresy. I also renounce and repudiate all false teachings that I have been taught by my ancestors, pastors, teachers, or friends. As one who has been delivered from the power of darkness and translated into the kingdom of Light, I cancel out all acts and effects these false teachings have had on my mind. Today, I acknowledge that these false teachings have caused me to promote separation, division, debate, and arguments. I see the ramifications these false teachings have brought upon my relationships. I am now willing to restore any relationship that You call me to reconcile. As one who has been born again and brought into the unity of the Life of Christ, I cancel every act of oppression Satan has introduced to me, my family, and to individuals, I have wounded with these false teachings. I announce to Satan and all his forces that Christ and the power of His shed blood have cleansed me from the sin of twisting God's Word for my benefit. I embrace the Truth of the importance of using the Word of God to build up the body of Christ. I choose this day to submit myself to the act of studying the Word of God, but only in the strength and power of Jesus Christ through the indwelling life of the Holy Spirit. I declare myself eternally and completely free from the sin of heresy. All this I do in the name and authority of the Lord Jesus Christ. Amen.

Envy

ஓ†ৎ

*"He is conceited and understands nothing;
but he has a morbid interest in controversial questions and
disputes about words, out of which arise envy..."*
(1 Timothy 6:4)

ENCOURAGEMENT: A man of envy has a resentful awareness of another's gains or blessings, joined with the overwhelming desire to possess what another has materially, socially, mentally, relationally, or spiritually. Envy is an act of rebellion against God, one who is trying to find fulfillment in people, places, or things rather than being content in a relationship with God. This very sin in Jesus' accusers led them to arrest Him (Matthew 27:18).

God does not want us speaking from want. He desires us to be content with whatever circumstance He has placed us in (Philippians 4:11). He even calls us to be well content with all of our weaknesses, insults from others, distresses, persecutions, and the challenges of difficulties (2 Corinthians 12:10). For He knows when we are experiencing weakness, we can then become strong. Being godly Christians is a means of great gain only when accompanied by contentment (1 Timothy 6:6). To be godly is to be content.

PRAYER

I pray, now, only in the power of the blood of the Lord Jesus Christ. I here and now renounce and repudiate the sin of envy. I also renounce my sinful desire of always wanting more. I choose now to accept all weakness, financial distress, persecutions, difficulties, and circumstances that You have chosen for me. I announce to Satan and all his forces that Christ and the power of His shed blood, have cleansed me from always wanting more. I embrace the Truth of the importance of being well content with whatever circumstances with which I am faced. I declare myself eternally and completely free from the sin of envy. All this I do in the name and authority of the Lord Jesus Christ. **Amen.**

Temptation of Murder

❦✝❧

"You lust and do not have; so you commit murder. You are envious and cannot obtain; so you fight and quarrel. You do not have because you do not ask."
(James 4:2)

ENCOURAGEMENT: Most likely, 99% of the Christians reading this is not guilty of killing another human being. However, Jesus removed the concept of murder from the physical realm, placing it into the intention of one's heart (Matthew 5:21-22). Well, that puts the 99% into the category of being "guilty" of murder and the 1% free from such a sin. Murder begins in the heart when a person loses respect for another human being. 1 John 3:15 tells us, *"Everyone who hates his brother is a murderer, and you know that no murderer has eternal life abiding in him."*

PRAYER

Dear Heavenly Father, I acknowledge the forgiveness You offered on the Cross through Jesus Christ. I believe in the power of forgiveness through the indwelling Holy Spirit. I know that I have no power to forgive and be forgiven on my own. I bring the reality of Your forgiveness into my life by choosing to embrace those who have hurt me. I renounce all bitterness, anger, contempt, hatred, and murderous thoughts or actions my flesh has displayed against _____ (name of a murder victim). I acknowledge my murderous thoughts as sin. I pray the power of the shed blood of Jesus over my mind and ask that you renew my mind through the power of the Holy Spirit who lives within me. As one who has been crucified and raised with Christ and now sits with You in heavenly places, I renounce any and every way in which Satan has used the sin of *murder to hold either the victim hostage and me. I declare myself eternally and completely free from the condemnation of my bitterness. All this I do in the name and authority of the Lord Jesus Christ. Amen.*

Bathing in Sin

❧✝☙

"Suffering wrong as the wages of doing wrong. They count it a pleasure to revel in the daytime. They are stains and blemishes, reveling (bathing) in their deceptions, as they carouse with you."
(2 Peter 2:13)

ENCOURAGEMENT: The expression of the sin of reveling involves orgies, carousing, enfeebling, indulgence, effeminacy, sensuality, and general sensual escapism. A person involved in reveling arrogantly speaks out with words of vanity with the intent of enticing fleshly desires by sensual thoughts, deeds, and words (see 2 Peter 2:18). Sexual joking is a classic example of Christians covertly revealing their enslavement to reveling. Even though Christians have been set free from the power of sin, many act as slaves of corruption, for by what a man is overcome, by this he is enslaved.

PRAYER

As a child of You, God, purchased by the blood of the Lord Jesus Christ, I here and now renounce and repudiate all the sins of reveling (taking great joy in sin) I have ever committed. I also renounce and repudiate all the sins of reveling that my ancestors have committed. As one who has been delivered from the power of darkness and translated into the kingdom of Your dear Son, I cancel out all the demonic work that has been inflicted upon me by the enemy. In the power of Jesus Christ, I cancel every act of oppression Satan uses to tempt me. I announce to Satan and all his forces that Christ became a curse for me when He hung on the Cross and that the sin of reveling has no hold on me. As one who has been crucified and raised with Christ and now sits with Him in heavenly places, I renounce any and every way in which Satan may claim false ownership of me. I declare myself to be eternally and completely signed over and committed to the Lord Jesus Christ. All this I do in the name and authority of the Lord Jesus Christ. Amen.

PRAYING FOR OTHERS

Warfare for Others

∞†∞

"For though we walk in the flesh, we do not war according to the flesh, for the weapons of our warfare are not of the flesh, but divinely powerful for the destruction of fortresses. We are destroying speculations and every lofty thing rose up against the knowledge of God, and we are taking every thought captive to the obedience of Christ."
(2 Corinthians 10:3-5)

ENCOURAGEMENT: We must learn to pray aggressive warfare prayers for family and friends we believe are struggling with bondage. Pray this prayer aloud when led to intercede for loved ones.

PRAYER

My dear heavenly Father, in the name of our Lord Jesus Christ, I bring before You in prayer (loved one's name) _____. I ask for the Holy Spirit's guidance that I might pray in the Spirit as You have taught me. I thank You, Father, that You have sovereign control over _____. I thank You for the qualities you have placed in _____. In the name of the Lord Jesus, and as a priest of God, I ask for mercy and forgiveness for the sins by which _____ has grieved You. I plead the sufficiency of the blood of Christ to meet the full penalty _____'s sins deserve. I claim back the ground of their life, which _____ has given to Satan by believing the enemy's deception. In the name of the Lord Jesus Christ, I resist all of Satan's activity to hold _____ in blindness and darkness. Exercising my authority, which is given to me in my union with the Lord Jesus Christ, I pull down the strongholds, which the kingdom of darkness has formed against _____. I smash, break, and destroy all those plans formed against *_____'s mind, will, emotions, and body. In prayer, I destroy the spiritual blindness and deafness that Satan keeps on _____. I invite the Holy Spirit of God to bring the fullness of His power to convict, to bring to repentance, and to lead _____ into faith in their Lord Jesus Christ and Savior. I cover _____ with the blood of the Lord Jesus Christ, and I break Satan's power to blind _____ to the Truth of God.*

Believing that You, Holy Spirit, are leading me, I claim _____ for You in the name of the Lord Jesus Christ, and I thank You for the answer to my prayer. In the name of Jesus, I joyfully lay this prayer before You in the worthiness of His completed work. **Amen.**

Marriages

❦✝❧

"Marriage is to be held in honor among all, and the marriage bed is to be undefiled; for fornicators and adulterers God will judge."
(Hebrews 13:4)

ENCOURAGEMENT: The enemy attacks marriages to destroy the order of the marriage of the Lamb. By standing in the power of God's doctrines in preserving marriage, we are standing in the everlasting covenant of Christ's marriage with the Church.

PRAYER

In the name of the Lord Jesus Christ and by the power of His blood, I pull down the walls, relationships, and barriers Satan and his kingdom are building between _____ (husband) and _____ (wife). I ask that You, Lord, demolish all the destructive strongholds the kingdom of darkness has been able to erect in their marriage. I ask You to unleash the mighty power of the loving heavenly Father on their relationship to make it all You want it to be. I ask the Holy Spirit to put within _____ (husband), as head of his home, the fruit of the Spirit: love, joy, peace, patience, kindness, goodness, faithfulness, gentleness, and self-control. By faith, I pray the healing power of the true and living God on any damage the enemy may have caused their marriage. I claim with and for them the victory You offer us through the power of the Cross. It is in the name of Jesus, I pray. Amen.

Family Life

✥

"Marriage is to be held in honor among all, and the marriage bed is to be undefiled; for fornicators and adulterers God will judge."
(Hebrews 13:4)

ENCOURAGEMENT: The enemy attacks marriages to destroy the order of the marriage of the Lamb. By standing in the power of God's doctrines in preserving marriage, we are standing in the everlasting covenant of Christ's marriage with the Church.

PRAYER

In the name of the Lord Jesus Christ and by the power of His blood, I pull down the walls, relationships, and barriers Satan and his kingdom are building between _____ (husband) and _____ (wife). I ask that You, Lord, demolish all the destructive strongholds the kingdom of darkness has been able to erect in their marriage. I ask You to unleash the mighty power of the loving heavenly Father on their relationship to make it all You want it to be. I ask the Holy Spirit to put within _____ (husband), as head of his home, the fruit of the Spirit: love, joy, peace, patience, kindness, goodness, faithfulness, gentleness, and self-control. By faith, I pray the healing power of the true and living God on any damage the enemy may have caused their marriage. I claim with and for them the victory You offer us through the power of the Cross. It is in the name of Jesus, I pray. Amen.

Prayer for Parents

☙✝☙

*"Brother will betray brother to death, and a father his child;
and children will rise up against parents
and cause them to be put to death."*
(Matthew 10:21).

ENCOURAGEMENT: If there were no evidence that this had been done, it would scarcely be "credible." The ties which bind brothers and sisters, parents and children together are so strong it could hardly be believed that division of sentiment on Christian subjects would cause them to forget these tender relations. Yet, history shows us this has been done often. If this is so, then how inexpressibly awful must be the malignity, by nature, of the human heart against Christianity! Nothing else but this dreadful opposition to God and his Gospel has ever has induced, or can ever induce, people to violate the most tender relationships and consign their best friends to torture, racks, and flames. It adds to the horrors of this: those put to death in persecution were tormented in the awful modes that human ingenuity could devise. They were crucified; thrown into boiling oil; burned at stakes; roasted slowly over coals; compelled to drink melted lead; torn into pieces by beasts of prey; covered with pitch, and set on fire. Yet, dreadful as this prediction was, it was fulfilled. Incredible as it seems, parents and children, husbands and wives were found wicked enough to deliver up each other to these cruel modes of death on account of attachment to the Gospel. Such is the opposition of the heart of man to the Gospel! This type of hostility is becoming more and more common in the family unit of today. Satan desires to destroy parent/child relationships because it will bring bitterness between the Parent (God) and His children (the Christian).

PRAYER

Loving and Holy God of our Lord Jesus Christ, I deliberately yield _____ and _____ as parents into Your loving hands of care and protection. I uphold the victory and name of the Lord Jesus Christ over them as protection against the plans of darkness to harm and destroy their children. I ask You to assign holy angels to protect and the sealing ministry of the Holy Spirit on _____ and _____ (parents' names) at all times. I recognize the enemy's effort to put on them a spirit of fear and terror of losing or hurting their children. I thank You for the love, acceptance, and forgiveness You have given them as parents. I reject the fearful unbelief that darkness is trying to use to control their emotions. I believe, this day, that You are going to supply them with the grace and mercy to walk them through the daily trials You allow to come before them. Again, I choose this day to yield them, their children, and their extended family members to You. I pray their family would experience the reality of Your care, love, and protection through the power of Your living Truth. Amen

Prayer for Children

☙✝❧

"He must be one who manages his own household well, keeping his children under control with all dignity."
(1 Timothy 3:4)

ENCOURAGEMENT: *Keeping his children under control* - this does not mean that his "children" should reveal oppressive behavior, whatever may be true on that point. It refers to "the father" being a serious man in his family; a man free from levity of character, and from silliness and uncertainty in his conversation with his children. It does not mean that he should be severe, stern, or gloomy, which are often mistaken for an oppressive father and are inconsistent with the proper spirit of a true father. He should be a serious and sober-minded man who maintains proper "dignity"; maintains self-respect, and whose behavior should be such as to inspire others with respect for him.

Our children are the living example and fruit of our devotion to the ordinances of God's holy commands – be fruitful and multiply. The enemy knows the children are the next generation of the manifested fruit of God. He works to consume their minds with the silliness of character and fleshly indulgences. We must pray for our children and the children of others who seem to be struggling with the deeds of darkness. Our devotion to praying for His children gives us the responsibility to care for the Body of Christ as a complete unit.

Note: Silliness of character does not mean the father is without lightheartedness. Having fun with your children is essential.

PRAYER

In the Mighty name of You, Lord, and by the power of Your blood, I come against any powers of darkness causing or intensifying the out-of-control behavior of (child's name)_____. I ask that You subdue all of the work of the enemy in this child's life. I ask You would chase away all the wicked and manipulative works of darkness the enemy uses against this child. I pray that you would manifest Yourself in and around _____'s life by bringing the fruit of the Holy Spirit. If there are any forms of rebellion, I renounce it in Jesus' name. I thank you for the plans You have for this child. I rejoice in Your perfect and just will for this child's life. I put their future in Your hands. I ask that You sovereignly direct and reveal to _____ Your life mission and plans for them. Grant to this child the wisdom to discern Your will and embrace it with the fullness of joy. Please give their parents the wisdom to lead them according to Your Divine purpose. Amen.

Prayer for Grandchildren

༒✝༒

*"Grandchildren are the crown of old men,
and the glory of sons is their fathers."*
(Proverbs 17:6)

ENCOURAGEMENT: Reciprocity - a relationship between people involving the exchange of goods, services, favors, or obligations; especially a mutual exchange of privileges between trading nations or recognition of licenses between states; of good in sustained family relationships. A long line of children's children is the glory of old age; a long line of ancestors is the glory of their descendants.

What all that means is the grandchildren are our nations, states, and local church governments. We need to be praying for the health, welfare, and spiritual stability of grandchildren. God is a God of blessing generations. Our prayers and supplications for our children's children, or those of our loved ones, establish our future states, nation, and churches. Pray boldly for the grandchildren of our generation!

PRAYER

In the blessed name of my Lord and Savior Jesus, I praise You for entrusting _____ and _____ (grandparents' name) to be grandparents. I pray they will accept all the responsibilities of the biblical model of grandparenting: godliness, protectiveness, prayerfulness, and alertness to the wiles (tricks) of the enemy. I ask that You assist them to sever all spiritual and generational claims the enemy may have come down through their biological families and ancestry. I ask that You would retain for them as grandparents the hope and future of all generational virtues and blessings that come directly from You. I intercede for them as a brother/sister in Christ to accept their God-ordained responsibilities as protectors of Truth and Righteousness. I look to Your sovereign Lordship and Shepherding to care for their grandchildren—even to the point of Salvation for any unsaved member. I pray You would fulfill the eternal plan that You have for their entire family. It is in Your Mighty Name that I pray. **Amen.**

Seeing Evil Images

✂†✃

"Set your mind on the things above, not on the things that are on earth. For you have died and your life is hidden with Christ in God. When Christ, who is our life, is revealed, then you also will be revealed with Him in glory. Therefore consider the members of your earthly body as dead to immorality, impurity, passion, evil desire, and greed, which amounts to idolatry."
(Colossians 3:2-5)

ENCOURAGEMENT: We think in word pictures, and the enemy is well aware of that. He is quick to tempt us to fix our minds on graven images, which promote fear and bondage. God gave us a simple technique to take care of this type of attack – setting our minds on things above. The following warfare prayer helps the believer do just that. If your child(ren) or another loved one, this prayer will boldly deliver the message to the enemy. Pray it as often as necessary. Rarely does the enemy quit on venues of attacks that have to do with graven imagery. Stay faithful and alert.

Society today is under a deluge of images – they're called "MeMe's" (pictures that make statements). The reason this modality is so effective is that we think in pictures.

PRAYER

It is Your face that I desire to see in my mind and heart. I pray for a renewed mind through the power of the shed blood of Jesus. I bind all workings of Satan, or his kingdom, who are putting faces in my mind or in the mind of _____ (the person you are praying for). I ask that You *command these wicked powers to leave our house, family, and specifically _____'s mind right now. I ask that you would send the presence of this force to leave upon Your command. I claim my life, home, and family for the divine purpose of Jesus Christ and the kingdom of God. Because of the power and authority, You have given me as a Christian, I stand against these powers of darkness and forbid them to work in our minds, home, and individual family members. I ask You, Heavenly Father, to station Your holy angels at every window, door, and gateway to this home. I pray for You to replace these graven images with thoughts and images of Your heaven. I renounce the fear that comes with these dark forces and ask that You would pour Your love over our minds and our home. Remind me to pray this as often as Your Spirit leads me to do so. I am a Child of the living God, and I am free to walk in the privileges of Heaven. I pray specifically in the name of Jehovah Rapha (You), the God who heals.* Amen.

Losing a Child

✽✝✽

Now may our Lord Jesus Christ Himself and God our Father, who has loved us and given us eternal comfort and good hope by grace, comfort and strengthen your hearts in every good work and word.
(2 Thessalonians 2:16-17)

ENCOURAGEMENT: There is no pain like that of a loss of a child in death or become missing. With this pain level, I believe it is most important to pray the following prayer each day during the first few months of grieving.

We live in a culture today where our youth are committing suicide at an alarming rate. Human trafficking is at its all-time high. And…worst yet, most of the humans that are trafficked are our children. Can you imagine the pain suffered by parents, grandparents, and family who have become victims of this demise? Let alone the grief of the children who are missing.

PRAYER

My dear loving Father of our Husband Jesus Christ, I deliberately yield _____ into Your loving hands of care, support, and protection. I uphold the victory and name of the Lord Jesus Christ over _____ as protection against the plans of darkness the enemy may have in store to harm or destroy _____. I ask You to assign holy angels to protect and to seal the ministry of the Holy Spirit on this child at all times. I recognize the enemy's effort to put on me a spirit of fear and terror of losing _____. I reject this fear and renounce all attacks this fear brings upon my mind. I thank You for the love You have given to me for _____. I know You will supply me with the portion of grace and mercy I will need to walk with You through a trial if You choose to allow one to come upon my child. I deliberately yield up my children, myself, and all of our family into the supernatural care and staying power of the true and living God. I know You are the giver and taker of all life, and You will not allow this child to be yielded over to injury, illness, violence, or death if it is not in Your divine will. I stand on Your will and not that of myself or the enemy. I rest in the sovereign control You have over this child and me. It is in the blessed name of THE Father I pray. **Amen.**

Prayer for Single Parents

☙✝❧

Honor widows who are widows indeed; but if any widow has children or grandchildren, they must first learn to practice piety in regard to their own family and to make some return to their parents; for this is acceptable in the sight of God.
(1 Timothy 5:3-4)

ENCOURAGEMENT: Those who have been put in a position of single parenting must consider leaning on family and friends for help and guidance – particularly if the children are without a "head of the home." Do not look at dependence as 3a failure but as an act of obedience.

PRAYER

Dear God, I acknowledge You as the Parent of all the living. I bring the burden of my role as a single parent to You for Your wisdom, strength, and sustaining courage. I resist all efforts the enemy may have to put on me attitudes of resentment and self-pity that would only further harm the child(ren) and me. I ask You, as the ultimate Parent, to guide and encourage me through Your Word. Please bring to me a mentor who will help me parent my children to the best of Your design and will. I choose to look to You for Your provision in all my personal and family needs. I hold the victorious name of my Husband, Jesus Christ, over my child(ren) and me, that we may walk in Your provided victory each day. Please assign Your holy, guarding, protecting angels to minister to us in our every need. Help me be loving and submissive to You, the church's leadership, and to all governing authority. Help me to trust You with my future and the future of my child(ren). Please help me to seek Your face first and believe that You will add everything I need when I need it. It is through Your divine nature, I pray. Amen.

Protection at Bedtime

☙✝❧

"By this, love is perfected with us, so that we may have confidence in the day of judgment; because as He is, so also are we in this world. There is no fear in love; but perfect love casts out fear, because fear involves punishment, and the one who fears is not perfected in love."
(1 John 4:17-18).

ENCOURAGEMENT: *There is no fear in love* - love is not an affection that produces fear. There is no fear in the love we have for a parent, a child, or a friend. If a man had perfect love for God, he would have no fear of anything; for what would he have to dread? He would have no fear of death, illness, or any other thing that tempts us to doubt God's everlasting purpose of love. It is guilt that makes people fear what is to come, but the believer who knows his sins are forgiven knows he is filled with the love of God. He can walk in this world fearing nothing but God Himself. He knows and embraces the fact that God is a God of the past, present, and future. He trusts the Redeemer with all possible harm the future may bring his way. Christians filled with love believe that God causes all things to work together for good (Romans 8:28). The angels in heaven have always loved God and one another; they have no fear, for they have nothing to dread in the future. This same love, which heaven functions by, is available to us in the form of the Holy Spirit. We must willingly accept this Truth and stand boldly in that promise. The following prayer helps parents who are struggling with the fear of losing a child to illness, harm, or even death.

Now the reality. Children, in general, do not understand this kind of love. Most adult authentic Christians don't. But, what they can know is that their parent(s) love them unconditionally. If your child is accustomed to seeing or hearing anger, shouting arguments, disappointment, and rejection, the child WILL interpret this as withholding love. That is what rejection is. When love is withheld, fear moves in like a storm. Usually, when children are found with unknown fears, it is a confession that there is love being withheld from the child. It is not always true, but it is common.

Being a child counselor for most of my career, I have discovered that the child's environment 2 hours before bed should be free from stress, loud noises, image stimulation, and eruptions of anger. What that means for the parents is that the home schedule needs to be adjusted to provide an environment of rest, particularly before bedtime. My recommendation? Read the word of God over them (bedtime stories) before you tuck them in. Pray this prayer when you are finished with storytime. If your child throws "fits" before bed, it will take three months to change this behavior. The child will find comfort in peace sooner or later.

PRAYER

Dear God, now I lay my child(ren) down to sleep; I pray their mind, will, and emotions to keep. I commit their mind, will, emotions, and body into the keeping, protective power of You, Lord Jesus. I pray the Holy Spirit would minister to them as they are sleeping. I bind and forbid any powers of darkness to tamper with any part of their souls, consciously or subconsciously, on any level. I ask that You would send holy angels from Your heaven to protect them, their rooms, possessions, and this house. I join You in Your stated truth that You are a provisionary Father who cares about my child(ren). I stand with You in Your victory and protection this day. It is in Your protective name that I pray. Amen.

Quarreling Between Children

ஒ†ஒ

Now flee from youthful lusts and pursue righteousness, faith, love and peace, with those who call on the Lord from a pure heart. But refuse foolish and ignorant speculations, knowing that they produce quarrels. The Lord's bond-servant must not be quarrelsome, but be kind to all, able to teach, patient when wronged,
(2 Timothy 2:22-24)

ENCOURAGEMENT: The more we follow that which is good, the faster and the further we shall flee from evil. Children, or adults, who quarrel, are competing for first place, and striving for first place is nothing other than fellowshipping with unfruitful works of darkness. See how often the apostle cautions against disputes in fruitless discussions, which shows that debate consists more in unbelief and practicing what is most common for the enemy. Training your children in exchange for truth without completion is the key – for it is God who gives the discovery of the truth, by his grace brings all of us to acknowledge it. Otherwise, our hearts would continue to rebel against it. This is why probing, pushing, and debating for Truth is the most fruitless act children can entangle themselves in.

Always remember. The parent's role is in planting seeds of Truth, not shoving it down their throats. Think about you as the parent. How long has it taken you to be "obedient" to the indwelling Holy Spirit? My guess is, most of your life. No seed sprouts life immediately. It first must be planted, die, and take hold through the fertile environment it was planted. If you have a child-resistant to hearing and obeying Truth, you might want to check your home environment. If it is indeed healthy, remember that new life, or obedience, takes time to sprout.

PRAYER

Dear God, I confess to You, my living God, that my frustration is sin. I renounce the fact the enemy seeks to devour my child(ren) through hostility and quarreling. Jesus, just as You have taught me, I know that the sinful flesh loves to start quarrels. Cause me to teach my children the biblical principles of overcoming their flesh with Your Word. I notice levels of hostility and fighting between them and know it could be a warning of spiritual powers of darkness seeking to control their hearts and minds. I pull down all intensifying influences of darkness, building walls, barriers, and hostility between You, me, and my child(ren). In the blessed name of Jesus, I forbid any of these powers of darkness to create contention, anger, hate, and fighting between my child(ren), me, and You. I ask that the lordship of Jesus would settle deep down into their souls and that the Holy Spirit would minister to them in ways only You can. I choose to celebrate Your ability to control my child(ren), me, and forces that may come against us. Cause us to have loving relationships with each other that are honoring to You. It is through the peaceful unity of Your life that I pray. Amen.

Child Fascination With Violence

☙✝❧

Therefore consider the members of your earthly body as dead to immorality, impurity, passion, evil desire, and greed, which amounts to idolatry.
(Colossians 3:5)

ENCOURAGEMENT: It is our duty to destroy ideations that are inclined to the world's things, the flesh and the devil. Putting to death or yield them to the power of the Cross is what it is all about. If we don't – we will be obsessed with evil and violence, a sin most common with fatherless children. We need to teach our children to oppose evil things continually. Do not assist the fascination by purchasing toys, videos, movies, etc., that promote violence. It would help if you did the opposite – keep dark imagery far from a child. If you don't, your child will find an occasion for sin, seek out lusts of the flesh, and form a love for worldly things, and worse yet, become a child of violence - which is idolatry. It is necessary to mortify (put to death) sins our children enjoy, or else, if we don't, they will morph into darkness. The Word of God changes the way we think and supports the rule of right reason and conscience over appetite and passion; therefore, read the Word to your children often.

PRAYER

Dear Father, I acknowledge that violence and cruelty are ways against Your perfect plan. I know the enemy loves drawing my child(ren) into the curiosity of evil. I stand against this in Jesus' name. I renounce all *the cleverness of the enemy in tempting my child(ren) to fascinate over the works and powers of darkness. I recognize the cultural focus on violence as an expression of the murderous ways of Satan's darkness. Loving Father, I bring You my concern for the tendency toward violence and cruelty that I see in my child(ren). In the blessed and holy name of Jesus and by the power of His Cross, I resist and renounce all powers of darkness seeking to rule and control _____. I stand firmly against them and ask that You command these forces to leave and to go where the Lord Jesus commands them to go. I ask that the Holy Spirit would replace these tendencies with love, joy, and peace. Fill the child(ren)'s thoughts with the mind of Christ. It is in the peaceful name of Jesus I pray. Amen.*

Attraction To Occult

෴†෴

"There shall not be found among you anyone who makes his son or his daughter pass through the fire, one who uses divination, one who practices witchcraft, or one who interprets omens, or a sorcerer, or one who casts a spell, or a medium, or a spiritist, or one who calls up the dead. "For whoever does these things is detestable to the LORD; and because of these detestable things the LORD your God will drive them out before you.
(Deuteronomy 18:10-12)

ENCOURAGEMENT: Run as fast as you can away from any form of witchcraft or divinations! Do not for any reason allow your children to read books, watch shows, play games, or any other manipulative form of Satanism that will eat away at your child's heart. Do not pray this prayer if you plan to continue to allow your child(ren) to tamper with forces of darkness! It will only set you and your child up for deeper harassment. These prayers are scripted to shake the foundation of the enemy – not tempt them.

The best way to view this is by helping someone get freed from addiction. Imagine providing healthy methods of redeeming them from the addition – and it worked. Then, at dinner time, you set the same substance of addition in front of them. Worse yet, you take your "fix" right in front of them. It is not only wrong; it is illogical. It also confesses hypocrisy.

When parents pray over their children to remove fear or anger while knowing the disruptive behavior is from graven imagery, but let the child gets up in the morning returning to their addiction (video games) – the parent is considered impotent.

Never pray prayers of deliverance without removing the items from the home that causes the behavior. It is that simple. However, this might require you as the parent to toss some idols out as well. Since most parents are not willing to do this, the cycle of darkness not only remains in your home it intensifies daily. Then one day, you wake up and ask yourself, *where did I go wrong?* Need I answer that question for you? Probably not.

Preparing your children for Christ-as-Life adulthood is in setting an example for the child when they are a child. Start today no matter what stage you are in with your child(ren).

PRAYER

Dear Jesus, I hate the occult with the very passions You have placed within my soul. I only love and cherish the sound and biblical elements of Your Word. I thank You for the direct warnings in Your Word against all occult and demonic activities. I will choose to carefully warn and protect my child(ren) against any interests in such evil things. I have seen an increased interest in _____'s life - a magnetic fascination with the spiritualistic realm, especially as it relates to _____ (state what you see). I stand in the name of Jesus against all powers of darkness that seek to influence and draw my child(ren) into these spiritualistic interests. I resist them in the name of my blessed Savior and Lord Jesus Christ. I pray that You would command the enemy and all of his followers to leave. Cause me to read and pray Your Word over my child(ren) daily. It is through Your perfect doctrines that I pray. Amen.

Early Sensual Attractions

⋙✝⋘

It is actually reported that there is immorality among you, and immorality of such a kind as does not exist even among the Gentiles, that someone has his father's wife.
(1 Corinthians 5:1)

PRAYER

Dear God, You are a covenant God who teaches us to lead our children in doctrines of pure Truth. I do thank You God that You have already chosen a life partner for _____. I pray for You to keep my child for that chosen one and keep him/her for _____. Thank You for hearing my prayer and concern for their sexuality. I ask that You work out the details in all their relationships and lead them into confessing with their mouths that You have a mate chosen for them – that they do not need to seek one. Your perfect time and way are what I desire for _____. I stand against any corrupting schemes the enemy may have in promoting relationships that will preoccupy their minds with the opposite sex or even the same sex. In Your name, I resist their efforts to rebel and go with the flow that the enemy has laid out for them. I pray for wisdom and understanding from Heaven as I attempt to lead them and guide them into the purity of Your doctrines. In prayer, I stand against all sexual impurities and temptations the enemy may attempt to bring into their relationships. I pray the pure doctrines over them. I pray this only in the name of the Purest name – Jesus Christ. **Amen.**

Child Sexual Perversions

✥

"I am afraid that when I come again my God may humiliate me before you, and I may mourn over many of those who have sinned in the past and not repented of the impurity, immorality and sensuality which they have practiced."
(2 Corinthians 12:21)

PRAYER

Dear God, I thank You for Your perfect and holy purpose for sexual desires. I pray in the name of Jesus against the perversion and misuse of Your gift of sexuality. Any form of perversions my child(ren) may be involved with I acknowledge as sin. Through the words, You put in my mouth, grant me the wisdom to convey to my child(ren) biblical values concerning their sexuality. In the name of Jesus and by the power of His shed blood, I resist and stand against all strongholds of sexual perversion the adversary has assigned to manipulate and rule over _____'s sexuality. I specifically resist strongholds of _____ (list specific tendencies you are aware of). I ask that You command the enemy from having access to my child(ren) in this area. I pray that You give my child(ren) the desire of purity and a willingness to save their body for righteousness. I humbly ask for protection over them, me, and others they may come in contact with. I stand willing to be Your vessel in Your name. **Amen.**

Out of Control Child

※ † ※

Children, obey your parents in the Lord, for this is right. HONOR YOUR FATHER AND MOTHER (which is the first commandment with a promise), SO THAT IT MAY BE WELL WITH YOU, AND THAT YOU MAY LIVE LONG ON THE EARTH.
Fathers, do not provoke your children to anger, but bring them up in the discipline and instruction of the Lord.
(Ephesians 6:1-4)

PRAYER

In the mighty name of my Lord and Savior Jesus Christ and the power of Your might, I come against all powers of darkness causing or intensifying the out-of-control behavior of _____ . I subdue the powers of darkness affecting this child with the blood of Jesus. I ask Lord that You calm this child's heart and mind with the supernatural power of the Holy Spirit. I ask that You command the enemy to cease from any forms of attack and wickedness that he may be bringing against _____ . I choose to believe in the Truth of Your deliverance. You own this child; the enemy has no right over their mind, will, or emotions. I pray that you chase away all evil and tendencies to curse me, our family, or You. Lord Jesus Christ, I ask You to manifest in _____ the spiritual fruit of self-control that comes from the Holy Spirit. Please give me the wisdom to manage _____ with the wisdom of heaven. Keep all selfish ambition out of my heart, and I pray that you keep me yielded to You as I help _____ embrace the Truth that will set him/her free. I pray in the name of Deliverance. **Amen.**

PRAYING FOR LEADERSHIP

Prayer for Leaders

"Obey your leaders and submit to them, for they keep watch over your souls as those who will give an account. Let them do this with joy and not with grief, for this would be unprofitable for you."
(Hebrews 13:17).

ENCOURAGEMENT: As they that must give account (to God) - The ministers of the Gospel must soon be called by God to give account for their walk in Christ, for all they teach, and for every measure which they adopt. Therefore, the best security is under the influence of the solemn truth that they will pursue only the course which will be for the good of the Body of Christ. That they may do it with joy, and not with grief – No sighing or groaning, as they would who had been unsuccessful. The meaning here is that leaders should lead with an attitude of joy and mastery over the enemy's influence. They need your prayers.

PRAYER

Dear heavenly Father, I come before You boldly on behalf of *Your servant* _____ *(leader's name). I cover this leader with the blood of the Lord Jesus Christ as protection during their time of prayer. I surrender* _____ *to You completely and unreservedly in every area of their life. I do take a stand against all of the workings of Satan that would hinder* _____ *from their prayer life. I ask that* _____ *address You as the only true and living God. I refuse any involvement of Satan in their leadership.*

Satan, the Lord Jesus commands you to leave this leader's presence with all of your demons. I bring the blood of the Lord Jesus Christ between you and ____/their leadership.

I pray that You, Lord Jesus, and the blessed Holy Spirit, would bring all the work of the crucifixion, all the work of the resurrection, all the work of the glorification, and all the work of Pentecost into ____'s life today. I surrender ____ to You. I renounce any and all discouragement, guilt, and condemnation from being in their heart and mind. I pray that You would release ____ to pray prayers of repentance as You lead.

You Lord, have proven Your power by resurrecting Jesus Christ from the dead. I claim in every way Your victory over all satanic forces that may be active in ____'s life and I reject these evil forces. I pray in the name of the Lord Jesus Christ with thanksgiving. I request that You would continue to form ____ into being a model of servant leadership. Please supernaturally protect all those under their care. Cause ____ to be gentle and full of grace. May their leadership be a reflection of Your life and leadership. It is only In Jesus' name I pray. **Amen.**

Prayer for Ministry

୨†ୡ

Giving no cause for offense in anything, so that the ministry will not be discredited, but in everything commending ourselves as servants of God, in much endurance, in afflictions, in hardships, in distresses."
(2 Corinthians 6:3-4).

ENCOURAGEMENT: Giving no offense in anything - The ministers of God should not render the Word of God to offense. "Offense" means: stumbling, falling into sin. The meaning here is giving no occasion for condemning or rejecting the Gospel. Paul's idea is that he and his fellow apostles so labored that no one who saw or knew them should have occasion to reproach their ministry or the Gospel they preached. Ministries need diligent prayer for the success of those who follow that ministry. Pray with a boldness that will shake the foundation of those who attempt to attack it.

PRAYER

Dear heavenly Father, Your divine revelations and guidance is needed for _____ (ministry name). Your ordained plan needs to be embraced on a day-to-day basis. I pray that You would empower the leadership of this ministry to accomplish Your will. I ask that the enemy would not have any entrance to this ministry in any way. I pray that You would cause the staff, volunteers, and trainees to walk according to Your Divine will and purpose. I ask that You would remove all self-ideas and supernaturally plant Your ideas, solutions, and counsel in their hearts and minds. I reject all forms of evil that may be "knocking" at their door. Cause them to function in the purity of Your financial provisions. Direct each leader to hear Your voice and to rebuff the rejection of man. I pray for Your empowerment to overwhelm them with Truth. Give them the heart of Jesus in all they do. Offer them discernment in each decision that needs to be made and deliver them from temptations to prosper in ways that do not bless You. Please give them the peace to sustain Your mission and purpose. Cause me to pray for them as You lead. Thank you for their love for the ministry and their hearts of compassion. Fill them with more of Your grace and compassion. It is in the blessed name of Jesus, I pray. **Amen.**

Affirmation Prayer

ଚ†ଚ

PRAYER

Today, I deliberately choose to submit myself fully to God, as He has made Himself known to me through the Holy Scriptures. I honestly accept His Word as the only inspired, infallible, authoritative standard for all life and practice. On this day, I will not judge God, His work, others, or myself.

1. *I recognize, by faith, that the true God is worthy of all honor, praise, and worship as the Creator, Sustainer, and End of all things. He is the Alpha and the Omega. I confess that God, as my Creator, made me for Himself. In this day, I, therefore, choose to live for Him.*
2. *I recognize, by faith, that God loved me and chose me in Jesus Christ before time began.*
3. *I recognize, by faith, that God has proven His love for me in sending His Son to die in my place, in whom every provision has already been made for my past, present, and future needs through His representative work. I have been quickened, raised, and seated with Jesus in the heavenly places and anointed with the Holy Spirit.*
4. *I recognize, by faith: God has accepted me since I have received Jesus Christ as my Lord and Savior; He has forgiven me; He has adopted me into His family, assuming every responsibility for me; He has given me eternal life; He has applied the perfect righteousness of Christ to me so that I am now justified; He has made me complete in Christ, and He offers Himself to me as my daily sufficiency through prayer and the decisions of faith.*

5. *I recognize, by faith, that the Holy Spirit has baptized me into the Body of Christ; sealed me; anointed me for life and service; seeks to lead me into a deeper walk with Jesus, and fills my life with Him.*

6. *I recognize, by faith, that only God can deal with sin and only God can produce holiness of life. I confess that my part was only to receive Him; He dealt with my sin and saved me. Now, I confess that to live a holy life; I can only surrender to His will and receive Him as my sanctification. I trust Him to do whatever may be necessary for my life, without and within, so I may be enabled to live in purity, freedom, rest, and the power for His glory.*

7. *For this day, I decide in faith to surrender wholly to the authority of God as He has revealed Himself in the Scripture – to obey Him. I confess my sin, face the sinful reality of my old nature (that is dead), and deliberately choose to walk in the Light, in step with Christ, throughout the hours of this day.*

8. *For this day, I decide in faith to surrender wholly to the authority of God as revealed in the Scripture – to believe Him. I accept only His Word as the final authority. I now believe that since I have confessed my sin, He has already forgiven and cleansed me. I accept at full value His Word of promise to be my sufficiency and rest, and I will conduct myself accordingly.*

9. *For this day, I decide in faith to recognize that God has made every provision so that I may fulfill His will and calling in my life. Therefore, I will not make any excuse for my sin and failure.*

10. *For this day, I make the deliberate decision of faith to receive from God the provision He has made for me. I renounce all self-effort in living the Christian life and performing God's service; I renounce all sinful praying that asks God to change circumstances and people so that I may be more spiritual; I renounce all drawing back from the work of the*

Holy Spirit within and the call of God without; and I renounce all non-biblical motives, goals, and activities which serve my sinful pride. I receive Jesus as my sanctification, my deliverance, my anointing, and my promise for daily living.

Victor In Christ

༄✝༄

"Now to Him who is able to keep you from stumbling, and to make you stand in the presence of His glory blameless with great joy, to the only God our Savior, through Jesus Christ our Lord, be glory, majesty, dominion and authority, before all time and now and forever. Amen" (Jude 1:24-25).

You are a victor in Christ Jesus! Don't ever forget this. The enemy will do all he can to have you consider this to be just another study. God has done mighty work in your heart and life. You are blameless in Christ, and you should embrace this Truth with a great deal of joy. Give God all the glory, majesty, dominion over your life, and authority to rule you each day. When you know the Truth, the Truth will set you free.

"Now may the God of peace Himself sanctify you entirely; and may your spirit and soul and body be preserved complete, without blame at the coming of our Lord Jesus Christ. Faithful is He who calls you, and He also will bring it to pass" (1 Thessalonians 5:23-24).

It is my daily prayer that God will give you His peace each day. I ask the Lord to sanctify you in every area of your life. I hope your spirit, soul, and body will be made complete and without blame until Jesus comes to greet us in His Second Coming. God is faithful in calling you to daily repentance and godly living. He will bring all of your struggles with the temptation to pass. This is a promise and commitment to you by the only living God.

"Now the God of peace, who brought up from the dead the great Shepherd of the sheep through the blood of the eternal covenant, even Jesus our Lord, equip you in every good thing to do His will, working in us that which is pleasing in His sight, through Jesus Christ, to whom be the glory forever and ever. Amen" (Hebrews 13:20-21).

The Lord's covenant (promise) with you comes through the seal of the blood of the eternal covenant of Jesus Christ. Because of this seal, He has equipped and empowered you to accomplish His will in your life. When you rest in the reality that God does this work through you, via the Holy Spirit who resides in you, He will be well pleased with all the efforts you apply in the Spirit. This promise, written in blood, will "seal the deal" in all of your warfare activities. We may be sheep, but He is the Lion of Judah!

"Now to Him who is able to do far more abundantly beyond all that we ask or think, according to the power that works within us, to Him be the glory in the church and in Christ Jesus to all generations forever and ever. Amen" (Ephesians 3:20-21).

I trust that you will dedicate all of your efforts to the One who can do for you more than you could ask or even think about asking. Your resources are limitless in Christ Jesus. Never fall into the trap of thinking that God does not care about the small or insignificant things in your life. He not only cares about these small things, but He reveals to us in the Word that those of us who are faithful in the small things, He will entrust much to them (see Luke 16:10).

"The grace of the Lord Jesus Christ be with your spirit" (Philippians 4:23).

It is my prayer that God's grace (unmerited favor) would be poured upon your spirit for daily living. As Satan tries to condemn you with feelings of guilt and condemnation, know that

God's grace is never going to change – no matter what you choose to do in walking after the flesh. Condemnation may be one of the major tools the enemy uses to keep you from walking in victory, but God's grace is what sustains you to face the lie and to walk in what is true about you.

"Take heed to the ministry which you have received in the Lord, that you may fulfill it" (Colossians 4:17).

God is not just interested in setting you free from the deeds of your flesh; He wants you to step into the ministry that He has called you to fulfill. That doesn't mean you have to quit your "job," but it certainly means that He wants to use your "job" to accomplish His mission for you and those around you. Consider praying about how God would want you to spread the Word of the Gospel into your daily living. It might mean going into full-time ministry, or it could mean one-on-one discipling of others of your gender, teaching Sunday school class, giving your testimony publicly, helping with a ministry you have come to love, or simply ministering to your family. Whatever it is, He wants you to fulfill it.

If you need help locating your calling, get together with an experienced discipler (biblical counselor) to aid you in discovering how you can give the life of Christ away in your daily living. This element of healing is critical for your ongoing growth as a believer.

"Diligently help Zenas the lawyer and Apollos on their way so that nothing is lacking for them. Our people must also learn to engage in good deeds to meet pressing needs, so that they will not be unfruitful" (Titus 3:13-14).

One of the easiest and most beneficial ways of reaching out to others in need is helping other ministry leaders accomplish the work God has called them. Find out what their pressing needs are, and then give time, effort, money, material possessions, skills, or whatever you have to offer. This way, the people and ministries you believe in can be fruitful and multiply the works of God. You and I must engage in good deeds to meet the pressing needs of God's ministry.

"Now may the Lord of peace Himself continually grant you peace in every circumstance. The Lord be with you all!" (2 Thessalonians 3:16).

As God allows circumstances to flood your world, cling to the peace that will surpass all of your understanding. You will find that this kind of peace will guard your heart and mind in Christ Jesus. He has already promised that He will be with you through it all. Therefore, press on to the mark of excellence. Don't look behind; just fix your eyes on Jesus, and He will direct you in all of your plans.

"Guard what has been entrusted to you, avoiding worldly and empty chatter and the opposing arguments of what is falsely called 'knowledge'-- which some have professed and thus gone astray from the faith. Grace be with you" (1 Timothy 6:20-21).

God wants you to put up a shield (guard) around the persons, places, and things He has entrusted to you, remembering that your shield is faith and faith without works is dead (James 2:22). Apply what you have learned and do not slip back into worldly discussions and arguments falsely called "knowledge." These friends or strangers claim to be wise in their own eyes, but their debating and wrangling of words have caused them to go astray from the faith. Avoid such men!

"But the Lord stood with me and strengthened me, so that through me the proclamation might be fully accomplished, and that all the Gentiles

might hear; and I was rescued out of the lion's mouth" (2 Timothy 4:17).

Jesus Christ has a mission to stand with you and strengthen you in all of your ways. He wants you to proclaim all of what He has shown you to others. This is how He accomplishes His divine will be for mankind. He wants all men to hear and experience the freedom they have been given. You were rescued; now help others be rescued!

"Having confidence in your obedience, I write to you, since I know that you will do even more than what I say" (Philemon 1:21).

Take great confidence in what God has done for you. Your obedience to complete this and other studies of the Lord is for a divine purpose. Many of you will accomplish far more than what I have as a servant of the Lord. One of the greatest privileges of being a minister is watching others embrace Truth and carry it far beyond the measurement initially given to me (minister/teacher).

"My brethren, if any among you strays from the truth and one turns him back, let him know that he who turns a sinner from the error of his way will save his soul from death and will cover a multitude of sins" (James 5:19-20).

I hope that we have been able to cover many of your sins with the grace of Jesus Christ. I trust that this study has brought you into a more dynamic relationship with Christ. This study does not offer a lifetime guarantee from insults, persecutions, difficulties, and distress. Christ, Himself doesn't even offer that. He warns us of suffering as He has suffered (1 Peter 2:19; 5:9; Acts 9:16; Romans 8:17). God is more interested in what we do with our sufferings. If we embrace the Truth that all things work together for good (Romans 8:28), we will not consider it strange when the enemy brings temptations and attacks our way.

Most stories of victory are birthed from pain, struggle, and perseverance. Your story is probably no different. I hope that your story is His story in the making.

-Dr. Stephen R. Phinney

Scriptural Helps

Faith

Hebrews 11:1
Now faith is the assurance of things hoped for, the conviction of things not seen.

Romans 10:17
So faith comes from hearing, and hearing by the word of Christ.

Romans 12:2
And do not be conformed to this world, but be transformed by the renewing of your mind, so that you may prove what the will of God is, that which is good and acceptable and perfect.

Matthew 17:20
And He said to them, "Because of the littleness of your faith; for truly I say to you, if you have faith the size of a mustard seed, you will say to this mountain, 'Move from here to there,' and it will move; and nothing will be impossible to you."

Romans 1:17
For in it the righteousness of God is revealed from faith to faith; as it is written, "BUT THE RIGHTEOUS man SHALL LIVE BY FAITH."

Hebrews 11:6
And without faith it is impossible to please Him, for he who comes to God must believe that He is and that He is a rewarder of those who seek Him.

Matthew 9:20
And a woman, who had been suffering from a hemorrhage for twelve years, came up behind Him and touched the fringe of His cloak; for she was saying to herself, 'If I only touch His garment, I

will get well." But Jesus turning and seeing her said, "Daughter, take courage; your faith has made you well." At once, the woman was made well.

Mark 9:23.
And Jesus said to him, "If You can? All things are possible to him who believes."

Love

1 John 4:10-12
In this is love, not that we loved God, but that He loved us and sent His Son to be the propitiation for our sins. Beloved, if God so loved us, we also ought to love one another. No one has seen God at any time; if we love one another, God abides in us, and His love is perfected in us.

John 15:9-10
"Just as the Father has loved Me, I have also loved you; abide in My love. If you keep My commandments, you will abide in My love; just as I have kept My Father's commandments and abide in His love."

John 14:21
"He who has my commandments and keeps them is the one who loves Me; and he who loves Me will be loved by My Father, and I will love him and will disclose Myself to him."

1 John 4:16, 21
We have come to know and have believed the love which God has for us. God is love, and the one who abides in love abides in God, and God abides in him. And this commandment we have from Him, that the one who loves God should love his brother also.

Jeremiah 31:3
The LORD appeared to him from afar, saying, "I have loved you with an everlasting love; Therefore I have drawn you with lovingkindness."

Romans 8:38-39
For I am convinced that neither death, nor life, nor angels, nor principalities, nor things present, nor things to come, nor powers, nor height, nor depth, nor any other created thing, will be able to separate us from the love of God, which is in Christ Jesus our Lord.

John 13:34-35
"A new commandment I give to you, that you love one another, even as I have loved you, that you also love one another. By this all men will know that you are My disciples, if you have love for one another."

Praise

Isaiah 43:21
The people whom I formed for Myself Will declare My praise.

1 Peter 2:9
But you are A CHOSEN RACE, A royal PRIESTHOOD, A HOLY NATION, A PEOPLE FOR God's OWN POSSESSION, so that you may proclaim the excellences of Him who has called you out of darkness into His marvelous light.

Hebrews 13:15
Through Him then, let us continually offer up a sacrifice of praise to God, that is, the fruit of lips that give thanks to His name.

Psalm 34:1

I will bless the LORD at all times; His praise shall continually be in my mouth.

Psalm 47:1-7
O clap your hands, all peoples; Shout to God with the voice of joy. For the LORD Most High is to be feared, a great King over all the earth. He subdues peoples under us and nations under our feet. He chooses our inheritance for us, the glory of Jacob whom He loves. Selah. God has ascended with a shout, The LORD, with the sound of a trumpet. Sing praises to God, sing praises; Sing praises to our King, sing praises. For God is the King of all the earth; Sing praises with a skillful psalm.

Psalm 48:1
Great is the LORD, and greatly to be praised, in the city of our God, His holy mountain.

Psalm 50:23
He who offers a sacrifice of thanksgiving honors Me; And to him who orders his way aright I shall show the salvation of God.

Psalm 63:3-5
Because Your lovingkindness is better than life, My lips will praise You. So I will bless You as long as I live; I will lift up my hands in Your name. My soul is satisfied as with marrow and fatness, And my mouth offers praises with joyful lips.

Obedience

1 Samuel 15:22
Samuel said, "Has the LORD as much delight in burnt offerings and sacrifices as in obeying the voice of the LORD? Behold, to obey is better than sacrifice, And to heed than the fat of rams."

Isaiah 48:18
If only you had paid attention to My commandments! Then your well-being would have been like a river, And your righteousness like the waves of the sea.

Jeremiah 7:23
But this is what I commanded them, saying, "Obey My voice, and I will be your God, and you will be My people; and you will walk in all the way which I command you, that it may be well with you."

John 14:15, 21
"If you love Me, you will keep My commandments. He who has My commandments and keeps them is the one who loves Me; and he who loves Me will be loved by My Father, and I will love him and will disclose Myself to him."

1 John 2:2-6
And He Himself is the propitiation for our sins; and not for ours only, but also for those of the whole world. By this we know that we have come to know Him, if we keep His commandments. The one who says, "I have come to know Him," and does not keep His commandments, is a liar, and the truth is not in him; but whoever keep His word, in him the love of God has truly been perfected. By this, we know that we are in Him: the one who says he abides in Him ought himself to walk in the same manner as He walked.

Colossians 3:22-24
Slaves, in all things obey those who are your masters on earth, not with external service, as those who merely please men, but with sincerity of heart, fearing the Lord. Whatever you do, do your work heartily, as for the Lord rather than for men, knowing that from the Lord you will receive the reward of the inheritance. It is the Lord Christ whom you serve.

Fleshly Mind

Proverbs 12:8
A man will be praised according to his insight, but one of perverse mind will be despised.

Proverbs 15:14
The mind of the intelligent seeks knowledge, but the mouth of fools feeds on folly.

Proverbs 16:9
The mind of man plans his way, But the LORD directs his steps.

Proverbs 17:20
He who has a crooked mind finds no good, and he who is perverted in his language falls into evil.

Proverbs 18:2
A fool does not delight in understanding, But only in revealing his own mind.

Proverbs 18:15
The mind of the prudent acquires knowledge, and the ear of the wise seeks knowledge.

Ecclesiastes 1:13
And I set my mind to seek and explore by wisdom concerning all that has been done under heaven. It is a grievous task which God has given to the sons of men to be afflicted with.

Ecclesiastes 1:16
I said to myself, "Behold, I have magnified and increased wisdom more than all who were over Jerusalem before me; and my mind has observed a wealth of wisdom and knowledge."

Ecclesiastes 1:17
And I set my mind to know wisdom and to know madness and folly; I realized that this also is striving after wind.

Grace

John 1:14
And the Word became flesh, and dwelt among us, and we saw His glory, glory as of the only begotten from the Father, full of grace and truth.

John 1:16-17
For of His fullness we have all received, and grace upon grace. For the Law was given through Moses; grace and truth were realized through Jesus Christ.

Acts 4:33
And with great power, the apostles were giving testimony to the resurrection of the Lord Jesus, and abundant grace was upon them all.

Acts 6:8
And Stephen, full of grace and power, was performing great wonders and signs among the people.

Acts 15:11
But we believe that we are saved through the grace of the Lord Jesus, in the same way as they also are.

Romans 6:14
For sin shall not be master over you, for you are not under law but under grace.

Romans 6:15
What then? Shall we sin because we are not under law but under grace? May it never be!

Romans 11:6
But if it is by grace, it is no longer on the basis of works; otherwise grace is no longer grace.

Romans 12:3
For through the grace given to me I say to everyone among you not to think more highly of himself than he ought to think; but to think so as to have sound judgment, as God has allotted to each a measure of faith.

Holy Spirit

Luke 11:13
"If you then, being evil, know how to give good gifts to your children, how much more will your heavenly Father give the Holy Spirit to those who ask Him?"

Luke 12:10
"And everyone who speaks a word against the Son of Man, it will be forgiven him; but he who blasphemes against the Holy Spirit, it will not be forgiven him."

Luke 12:12
"For the Holy Spirit will teach you in that very hour what you ought to say."

Acts 2:4
And they were all filled with the Holy Spirit and began to speak with other tongues, as the Spirit was giving them utterance.

Acts 2:33
Therefore having been exalted to the right hand of God, and having received from the Father the promise of the Holy Spirit, He has poured forth this which you both see and hear.

Acts 2:38
Peter said to them, "Repent, and each of you be baptized in the name of Jesus Christ for the forgiveness of your sins; and you will receive the gift of the Holy Spirit."

Acts 4:31
And when they had prayed, the place where they had gathered together was shaken, and they were all filled with the Holy Spirit and began to speak the word of God with boldness.

Acts 7:51
You men who are stiff-necked and uncircumcised in heart and ears are always resisting the Holy Spirit; you are doing just as your fathers did.

Faithfulness

Romans 3:3
What then? If some did not believe, their unbelief will not nullify the faithfulness of God, will it?

Galatians 5:22
But the fruit of the Spirit is love, joy, peace, patience, kindness, goodness, faithfulness.

Luke 12:42

And the Lord said, "Who then is the faithful and sensible steward, whom his master will put in charge of his servants, to give them their rations at the proper time?"

Luke 16:10
"He who is faithful in a very little thing is faithful also in much; and he who is unrighteous in a very little thing is unrighteous also in much."

Luke 16:11-12
"Therefore if you have not been faithful in the use of unrighteous wealth, who will entrust the true riches to you? And if you have not been faithful in the use of that which is another's, who will give you that which is your own?"

Luke 19:17
"And he said to him, 'Well done, good slave, because you have been faithful in a very little thing, you are to be in authority over ten cities.'"

1 Corinthians 10:13
No temptation has overtaken you but such as is common to man; and God is faithful, who will not allow you to be tempted beyond what you are able, but with the temptation will provide the way of escape also, so that you will be able to endure it.

1 Thessalonians 5:24
Faithful is He who calls you, and He also will bring it to pass.

Bride of Christ

1 Corinthians 14:12
So also you, since you are zealous of spiritual gifts, seek to abound for the edification of the church.

Galatians 1:13
For you have heard of my former manner of life in Judaism, how I used to persecute the church of God beyond measure and tried to destroy it.

Ephesians 1:22
And He put all things in subjection under His feet, and gave Him as head over all things to the church.

Ephesians 3:10
So that the manifold wisdom of God might now be made known through the church to the rulers and the authorities in the heavenly places.

Ephesians 3:21
To Him be the glory in the church and in Christ Jesus to all generations forever and ever. Amen.

Ephesians 5:23
For the husband is the head of the wife, as Christ also is the head of the church, He Himself being the Savior of the body.

Ephesians 5:24
But as the church is subject to Christ, so also the wives ought to be to their husbands in everything.

Ephesians 5:25
Husbands, love your wives, just as Christ also loved the church and gave Himself up for her.

Ephesians 5:27
That He might present to Himself the church in all her glory, having no spot or wrinkle or any such thing; but that she would be holy and blameless.

Stewardship

Matthew 6:20-21
"But store up for yourselves treasures in heaven, where neither moth nor rust destroys, and where thieves do not break in or steal; for where your treasure is, there your heart will be also."

Matthew 6:33
"But seek first His kingdom and His righteousness, and all these things will be added to you."

Matthew 19:29
"And everyone who has left houses or brothers or sisters or father or mother or children or farms for My name's sake, will receive many times as much, and will inherit eternal life."

Luke 6:38
"Give, and it will be given to you. They will pour into your lap a good measure-- pressed down, shaken together, and running over. For by your standard of measure it will be measured to you in return."

LIFE MISSION:

Dr. Phinney is the Founder and Ministry Host of the Institute Of Ministry (IOM America), Identity Matters Worldview Institute, and the IM Online Worldview School.

Stephen & Jane have been married for over 40+ years and have three grown children: Abigail (husband, Quintin Eason), Elizabeth (husband, Nathan Ford), and Jessica. Jane & Steve have also been blessed with many grandchildren. They are dedicated to the institution of marriage, multigenerational family development, and local multigenerational family church development and advancing the believer's identity in Christ globally. Dr. Phinney is a pastor of a local church – XL-Church. A fellowship that focuses on the believer's indwelling union in Christ.

Stephen has authored multiple books/teaching series on spiritual growth and has published a plethora of articles/booklets assisting others in obtaining a Transformational Biblical Worldview. Visit, IOMAmerica.net

Even though he does NOT put much stock in these degrees, he holds a Bachelor's degree in Psychology, Masters's in Counseling Psychology, and a Doctorate in Ministry.

His Vison

Christ, Culture, and Creator. Compassion in Action. Helping members of the body of Christ to experience, mature in, and communicate the message of identification with Christ in His death, burial, resurrection, and ascension in the believer's various spheres of influence effectively.

He confesses that worldview is birthed through personal identity! This is why it is critical for his readers first to understand who they are in Christ before leading another in such a discovery. With this in mind, he aims to integrate the identification truths into all aspects of ministry communication. It is his experience that if any ministry or its workers focus on worldview issues before they gain an experiential understanding of the power of the Cross, these workers could lead the Church away from the Truth that should set them free. Understanding the power of the Cross, these workers could lead the Church away from the Truth that will set them free.

Because Jesus is Truth, his ministry diverts all students away from using Biblical truths as a way to perpetuate the wisdom of Christ who doesn't necessarily claim His indwelling Life. Most "Christian" worldview institutions tend to systematically explain the basic concepts of His Truth, existence, reality, and freedom, but shy away from the Supremacy of His indwelling promise - living through the believer. Dr. Phinney avoids this modality at all cost.

FURTHER READING & VIEWING:

All located at **IOMAmerica.net**

- IOM Research Publications
- Dr. Phinney's published books
- Weekly published online articles
- IM Blog Spot. Host to multiple authors
- Dr. Phinney's Eschatology Series
- Dr. Phinney's weekly church messages
- IM Worship Center | Featuring Don Moens
- IM-Home Churches
- IM Media Center
- IM Exchanged Life Bookstore
- IM eBookstore
- IMGabTV Channel
- IM Online Worldview School
- iPhinnity Art Gallery
- IM Pictorial Hebrew
- My Heart Undressed | Jane M. Phinney Blog
- Living Hope Ministries
- IM FlipBooklets
- And, much more…

Most Popular Book by the Author:

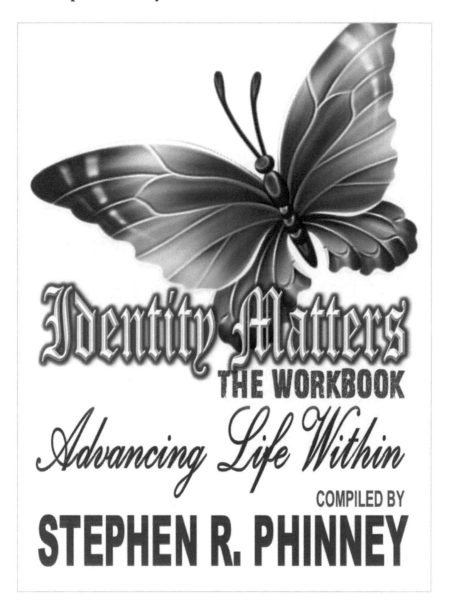